SECOND EDITION • REVISED AND EXPANDED

# Jazz Improvisation:
# The Goal-Note Method

A COMPREHENSIVE, PROGRAMMED GUIDE
TO JAZZ THEORY AND IMPROVISATION
## by Shelton Berg

**U.S. $42.00**
REPLACEMENT CD AVAILABLE @ $12.00

*"We don't create, it's already there . . .*
*We just choose."*


George Balanchine

To Gordon, my brother,
whose radiance is inextinguishable in my life.

# Acknowledgements

First of all I must acknowledge my mentors; who include my father and mother, Albert Hirsh, Jimmy Ford and Arnette Cobb, along with my earlier teachers, Maxine Priest and Lucien LeMieux. I am indebted to my literary advisor, Dr. Michael Horvit, and I appreciate the guidance of Dr. Tom Benjamin and Kenneth Neidig. Next there are the colleagues with whom I developed my playing; Tom Cummings, Larry Slezak, Bob McGrew, Tony Campise, John Park, Larry Martinez and many others. I am indebted to Bill Watrous for believing in me, and Lou and Cindy Fischer for believing in this project. My sincere thanks to Dick Dunscomb for providing so much inspiration by example. I also express gratitude to Rich Matteson and Jamey Aebersold, whose methods have served as a basis for my own. My children, Linsday, Kyle and Ashlyn, have supplied me with ample motivation for my work, and my brothers, sister, and in-laws have each inspired me in unique ways. And finally I must thank my students, whose probing questions created the atmosphere which resulted in the development of *The Goal-Note Method*.

# Preface

*Jazz Improvisation: The Goal-Note Method* is intended as a programmed text for a 2-4 semester improvisation program. The approach is consonance-based, emphasizing structural pitches and harmonic considerations as opposed to scale-derived melody. The premise of the book is that when consonant tones are surrounded with characteristic jazz formula (cliché), successful improvisation results.

The primary stylistic focus of the text is on be-bop and post-bop melodic idioms, in that these styles are the basis for most improvisation today. Harmony is presented with chord functions in mind. Chords are not viewed as separate entities, but rather with respect to their relationship to other chords (harmonic idioms). The book is structured to be studied in succession, with each chapter presenting material that is built on the preceding chapters.

In presenting the course, two procedures are advised. First of all, students should be encouraged to play often and in as uninhibited a manner as possible. The study of improvisation has become so theoretical that it threatens to stifle the creative aspect of the art. The development of an inventive style is directly linked to a vast amount of playing experience. And secondly, students must be taught to listen. Regardless of how much one studies and analyzes, improvisation is fundamentally an imitative art, and the language is assimilated through listening. It is advisable for each class to begin with the students listening to a classic jazz performance. As teachers we must create the frame of reference upon which our students will build their aspirations.

# Foreword
# to the 2nd Edition

The author, Shelly Berg, is a tremendous jazz musician and educator. The musical results he has achieved, first at San Jacinto College and now at the University of Southern California (USC), are spectacular. This new edition allows the reader to gain a clear insight into improvisation techniques that are being successfully used at many major jazz schools throughout the U.S.A.

*The Goal-Note Method* clearly assigns priorities that result in beginning improvisers of all ages sounding hip in a very short period of time. The early use of jazz nuances also reinforces authentic-sounding solos even if they are quite simple in the beginning. Learning the use of space is also a winner. The book continues through many logical steps that allow the student to progress with confidence and security.

This second edition contains three additional chapters that help to summarize and make even clearer the directions. Greatly expanded musical examples and a new play-along CD also enhance this offering.

Shelly Berg learned his improvisational skills by going to the jazz clubs, a method that is no longer feasible. His keen intellect, his superb musicianship, and his astute teaching skills combine to provide the next best option: *Jazz Improvisation: The Goal-Note Method*.

J. Richard Dunscomb
Director of Jazz Studies at
Florida International University
and American Coordinator
of the Montreux Jazz Festival

# Table of Contents

# Section 5: Appendices

# SECTION 1

# Introduction

CHAPTER 1

# General Style

## Be-Bop Melodic Construction

Melodies in the be-bop style tend to exhibit the following common characteristics:
1. Predominant eighth-note motion, with some triplets (although repeated alternation between one-beat triplet and 8th-note figures is *not* characteristic).
2. Unpredictable phrase lengths and unexpected phrase placement within the chord structure.
3. Off-beat beginnings and endings to phrases.
4. Combination of *lick* and line (see page 7).
5. Frequent use of syncopation (i.e. an off-beat eighth note followed by a rest, or a note longer than an eighth, off the beat. See Example 1.1, mm. 2 and 4).
6. Lines "turn around" on themselves.  This is accomplished through melodic skips, usually off the beat, balanced by step-wise motion in the opposite direction.
7. Numerous accented notes, most often off the beat, in unpredictable patterns.

Example 1.1 depicts a typical be-bop melody, as characterized above.

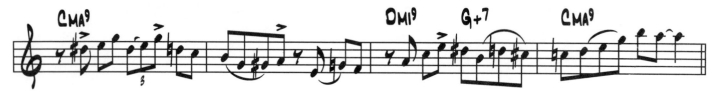

**Ex. 1.1  Characteristic jazz melody**

## 'Swing' Eighth Notes

Eighth notes in the jazz style are interpreted as follows:
1. Rhythm is triplet-like, where the first eighth-note of a beat retains two-thirds of the value of that beat.
2. The notes are played in a legato style.  If the note on the beat is played staccato, the "Lawrence Welk" effect results (i.e. a hokey, non-swinging style).
3. Accents, when they occur, are most often off the beat.
4. The rhythm tends to "straighten out" towards even note values as the tempo increases.  At very fast tempos, eighth-notes are all of equal length.

Example 1.2 shows the notation of jazz eighth-notes, and how they actually would be performed.

**Ex. 1.2  Notation and performance of "swing" eighth notes**

**Formula: Licks** • A *lick* is a short, melodic cell (motive), usually containing syncopation and made memorable by it's repetition.  A lick will rarely be more than one measure in duration.  Licks are often altered for variety, or to reflect new notes as the chords change.  They usually occur at the beginning of phrases, and can grow into be-bop lines. Example 1.3 shows a lick and its typical usage.

**Ex. 1.3  Lick and usage**

Remember: the eighth-notes in the example above are played in the swing style.

## Time

The most important component of an improviser's performance is the conveyance of tempo and rhythm, which can be referred to as *time*.  It is absolutely essential that the time emanate from the soloist, and not be left up to the rhythm section alone.  Improvisation should be practiced with the metronome in order to develop a strong sense of time (note: the metronome clicks should represent beats two and four of the measure).

When a performer accents the off-beat notes strongly and frequently, he is said to play with a *hard swing*.  A more subtle accentuation results in a *cool* style.  The character of an improviser is determined by his place in the spectrum between hard and cool playing.  In either case, the sense of time is obvious in the playing of a proficient improviser.

**Formula: Off-beat Starts and Endings** • As stated above, jazz phrases regularly begin one eighth-note before or after a beat.  The off-beat phrase ending can be on a long or short note value, as was depicted in measures 2 and 4 of Example 1.1.

## Exercises

1. Compose three licks, none longer than a measure, as described above.
2. Write a 4-bar be-bop melody displaying the characteristics outlined in this chapter.  Be sure to include accent markings to indicate performance style.
3. Bring a recording to class in which you can indentify specific licks and typical be-bop melodic idioms.
4. Play Exercises 1 and 2 in class.
5. Practice "matching pitch" by repeating on your instrument, by ear, single notes or short motives performed by the instructor.

CHAPTER 2

# The Goal Note Method

## Consonance

The Goal Note Method of jazz improvisation is based upon a centuries-old principle of melodic structure. Simply stated, the idea is that melody is held together by placing *consonant tones* (i.e. chord tones) on the important beats. A good melody, therefore, is not based on a series of scales, but rather on emphasizing the notes of the chords in the progression. The goal of the improvised line is to pass through these consonant tones on the way to a final chord tone (goal note) at the end of the line. Certain consonant tones should be used more frequently than others in order to clearly outline the chords. Jazz musicians call this "playing the changes." The hierarchy of consonant tones in a chord is, in most instances, as follows:

1. 3rd and 7th
2. root and 5th
3. 9th and 13th (6th)
4. ♯11th (♭5th) for major and dominant chords,
   11th for minor and half-diminished chords
5. altered tones -- ♭9, ♯9, ♭13 (♯5) -- for dominant chords

There are some important observations for dealing with goal notes. These are:

1. Arpeggio is more important than scale as a melodic generator, especially when you consider that a 13th chord with an 11th contains seven tones, the same number as in a major or minor scale! It is far better to think of these tones in their chordal alignment.
2. Many scales can be constructed by simply filling in the space between successive chord tones. The combinations are far less limited than would be achieved using conventional scales. A scale, then, can be defined as chord tones and notes in between.
3. All twelve tones are valid in an improvised line, as long as consonant tones are on the principle beats.
4. Melodic skips tend to accentuate the notes involved. Therefore, skips are normally made from or to a chord tone. When a line skips into a non-chord tone, the next move is usually by step to a chord tone.
5. Successive skips to non-chord tones are almost always incorrect because the wrong chord is being arpeggiated.
6. The last note of a line is the most important. If the note is highly consonant, it will validate what comes before it.
7. Very often the last note of a phrase is the third of the chord.

Example 2.1 shows a major scale, which "works" melodically due to the placement of the consonant tones. The example also contains a hybrid scale, which works more effectively, based on the same chord tones.

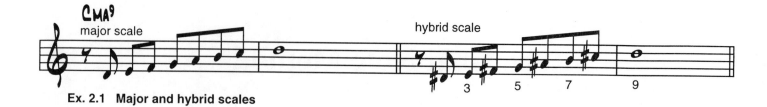

**Ex. 2.1  Major and hybrid scales**

The following examples demonstrate the fact that scales alone are not sufficient to insure successful jazz melody.  Example 2.2 is from the "Sonata in C Major, K545" for piano by W. A. Mozart.

**Ex. 2.2  Mozart sonata**

It might be assumed that this melody is successful because it employs all tones in the C major scale, the preferrable scale for these chords.  However, if this were true, then Example 2.3 would be equally viable.

**Ex. 2.3  "Wrong note" Mozart**

If you play Example 2.3 with the chords, you find that, of course, the melody does not work at all!  The reason is that, although the tones are from the correct scale, they are not consonant against the prevailing chords.

Example 2.4 further illustrates the importance of goal notes.  This excerpt contains many tones which are not in the C major scale.  The tune is, in spite of the "wrong" notes, quite successful because it adheres to the principle of consonance on the important beats.

**Ex. 2.4  Embellished Mozart**

## Formula

As stated above, the premise of this book is that melody is based on a high degree of consonance, a theorum applicable to melody in general throughout the past several centuries. Equally important is to note that formula determines the appropriateness of a melody within a given style.

A *formula* is a melodic idea or device so idiomatic to the style that all jazz players use it frequently as a component of improvisation.

The study of improvisation then can be described as first learning to play the consonant tones, and then learning to surround these tones with idiomatic formulae. These formulae must be practiced diligently and inserted into the improviser's frame of reference. In this way, improvisation can be compared to choreography. When a ballet is created, the choreographer does not invent new steps, leaps and turns, but rather puts together existing ones into a new dance. Similarly, a jazz solo is not the creation of new melodic ideas, but simply the ordering of existing ideas into a new solo! This indicates that jazz improvisation can be practiced by specific means.

Example 2.5 shows the effect of formulae on melodic character. In this example, a set of consonant tones (goal notes) is surrounded by differing formulae to create melodies characteristic of three different periods in music history.

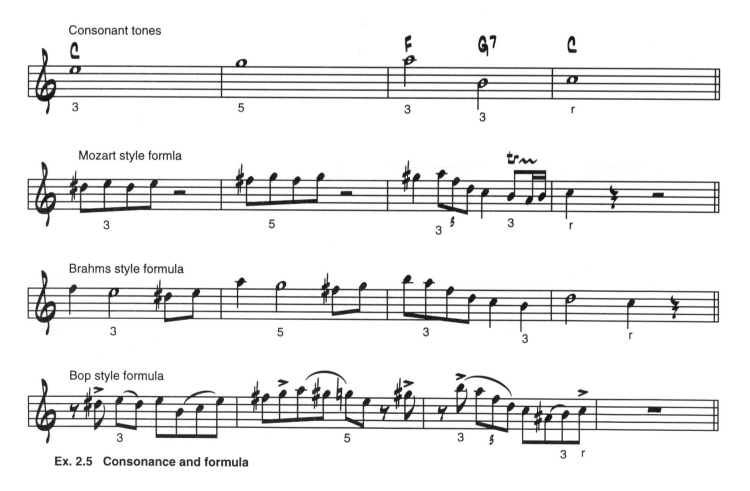

**Ex. 2.5 Consonance and formula**

Example 2.5 illustrates the fact that consonance has not changed considerably over the centuries, but formula has.

## Functional Harmony

One final concept that is fundamental to this study is the idea that chords are related to each other, and that chords in a progression have functions. This idea of functional harmony is essential to the study of classical music theory as well. Jazz is not a departure from classical music, but rather an outgrowth of it. Therefore, as chords in this book are studied, they will always be described in terms of function and placement within the progression. The result of this perspective will be to link various songs together as they share common harmonic ideas.

**Term: Changes** • The *changes* (or chord changes) are the actual chords in the progression of a song. The essential obligation of the improviser is to play the chord tones at the correct linear points, this creating the consensus that he is *playing the changes.*

### Exercises

1. Compose melodies employing the goal-notes provided below. Use princinples of jazz rhythm, accent, and phrasing. Play your melodies in class. [Note: This is an experiment in the goal-note method. Although the chords below have not yet been studied, acceptable melodies may result from using these goal notes. Treat this as a first attempt, and realize that you will become more proficient with melody in the subsequent weeks.]

CHAPTER 3

# Practice Techniques

## Practice Sheet Method

In order to improvise effectively to the chord changes, the student must first be acquainted with the basic components of the chords themselves. A practice-sheet method can be devised to facilitate this task. The *practice sheet* is a notation of the chords and scales contained in the progression of a song. Example 3.1 depicts two measures of a practice sheet, assuming that the chords change at a rate of one per bar. [Note: Jazz tunes are normally practiced in a range between 108 and 176 bpm. Set the metronome to half speed and think of the clicks as beats two and four.]

**Ex. 3.1  Practice sheet**

The practice sheet can be used in the following manner. Always playing in rhythm, and with the metronome, the student should perform the following tasks throughout the entire progression of the song:
1. Play the melody of the song.
2. Play the roots of each chord.
3. Play the roots and thirds.
4. Play the thirds and sevenths.
5. Play the arpeggios.
6. Play the scales best suited to the chords.
7. Practice a prescribed formula for each chord.

Example 3.2 on the following page demonstrates two bars of a practice-sheet method, employing steps 2 through 6 above. [Note: It is helpful to practice scales with varying patterns of accent. For instance, each off-beat note can be accented, or any single, off-beat note, or any combination in between.]

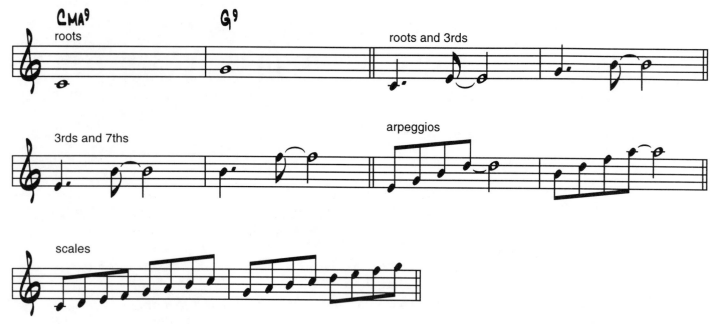

**Ex. 3.2   Practice sheet method**

**Practicing Inversions** • The practice-sheet method is helpful to the study of jazz improvisation, but it is not sufficient, in and of itself, as a means for mastering the chords.  A chord can be arranged with any of its notes on the bottom, giving rise to several *inversions*.  If the third of the chord is on the bottom, it is referred to as being in *first inversion*.  Second inversion has the chord-fifth as the lowest note, third inversion begins with the seventh, and so on.  By practicing all of the inversions in more than one octave, the improviser can learn a chord throughout the entire range of his instrument.

Example 3.3 demonstrates a practice method for inversions.

**Ex. 3.3  Practicing inversions**

Example 3.4 shows another permutation for arpeggio practice.  The root of the chord is not present in this exercise.  Most chords studied in this book will contain extensions of at least a ninth, allowing for this omission of the root in arpeggiation.  This practice is desirable and will be discussed later.

**Ex. 3.4  Practicing inversions (root omitted)**

3.3

When practicing inversions as previously outlined, bear in mind that there are only twelve different major ninth chords, and likewise minor ninths and dominants. Therefore, practicing C major ninth as in Example 3.4 is more than just an exercise towards learning a particular song. It represents the process of mastering one-twelfth of the possible major ninth chords! In this manner, all chords can be mastered in a relatively short period of time.

**Two Chords per Measure** • Obviously chords do not always change at a rate of one per bar. It is fairly common for them to move twice as quickly. In this case, certain adjustments must be made to the practice-sheet method. Example 3.5 shows a modification of steps 2 through 5 above.

**Ex. 3.5   Practice sheet method (2 chords per bar)**

With reference to scales, the adjustment involves more than simply altering rhythms. If two different scales are needed in one measure, then a combined scale/arpeggio can be played for each. Example 3.6 demonstrates the scale/arpeggio combination, using scale degrees 1, 2, 3 and 5 for each chord.

**Ex. 3.6   Combined scale/arpeggio**

If two chords in one measure share the same scale, then the above modification is not necessary. Example 3.7 depicts an instance of two chords sharing one scale.

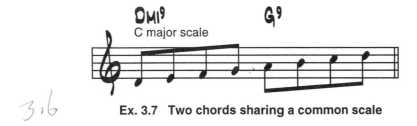

**Ex. 3.7   Two chords sharing a common scale**

One last modication of the practice-sheet method can be helpful. When two arpeggios are played in the same measure, a smoother progression results from inverting the second chord so that the bottom notes are close together, a process referred to in this text as *smooth arpeggiation*. Example 3.8 demonstrates chord inversion, as applied to the second chord in a measure.

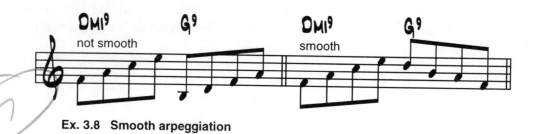

**Ex. 3.8  Smooth arpeggiation**

[Note: It is critical for the improviser to memorize all aspects of a practice sheet. This *internalization* is part of the process that transfers the melodic and harmonic materials into the ear. There is an axiom that says, "hear it, play it." In other words, in order for an improviser to perform a melodic idea, it must first *be* an idea, and ideas reside within the internal memory of the brain.]

# SECTION 2

# Primary Chord Types

CHAPTER 4

# Major Seventh (Ninth) Chords
## X$_{MA}$⁷

variant symbols: X$^{\Delta}$, X$^{\Delta7}$, X$_{maj}$⁷, X⁷̶

## Construction

The major seventh chord can be constructed by selecting the 1st, 3rd, 5th, and 7th notes of a major scale. The chord contains a major triad and a major seventh above the root. When a ninth is added, it is a major ninth (an octave and one whole step above the root). Example 4.1 displays the C major seventh and major ninth chords.

**Ex. 4.1   Major seventh and ninth chords**

[Note: In jazz it is most common to use ninth chords where seventh chords are indicated. When arpeggiating, the root can be omitted and replaced with the ninth. In this instance the root is still being heard, however, because it is played by the bassist in the group. On the other hand, it is not unacceptable to arpeggiate with the root, and the note itself can be very declamatory in a solo.

Example 4.2 shows the names of the chord tones, which are, from bottom to top, root, third, fifth, seventh, and ninth.

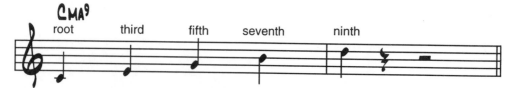

**Ex. 4.2   Names of the chord tones**

The seventh (7th) and ninth (9th) of the chord are each a diatonic step away from the root, and therefore serve to "frame" it melodically. Example 4.3 displays a common melodic gesture in which the arpeggio "frames" the root of the major seventh chord.

**Ex. 4.3  Arpeggio "framing" the chord root**

## Function

**Tonic** • In that the major seventh chord is constructed over the first note of a major scale or major key, it is generally considered to have *tonic function.* This means that it is the "home" chord, or the primary chord of a key. When functioning in this way, the major seventh chord is referred to as the tonic chord or the "one" chord, using the Roman numeral one (I). A song will usually begin and almost always end on the tonic (I) chord. Example 4.4 shows a short phrase beginning and ending on the tonic chord.

**Ex. 4.4  Phrase beginning and ending on tonic harmony**

**Scale** • A major seventh or major ninth chord functioning as tonic will employ the major scale of the chord root (i.e. CMA9 uses a C major scale; see Example 4.5).

**Ex. 4.5  Major scale for MA7 harmony**

**Sub-dominant** • In a major key, if a seventh chord is constructed above the fourth note in the scale it will also be a major seventh chord. In this usage, the chord is designated as the "four" chord (IV) or sub-dominant harmony. This function is fairly common, although much less frequent than tonic function among major seventh chords. Example 4.6 depicts the tonic (I) and sub-dominant (IV) chords in a major key.

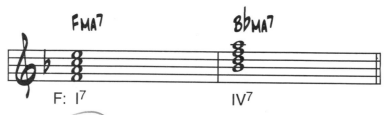

**Ex. 4.6  Tonic and subdominant chords**

**Scale** • A major seventh (9th) chord functioning as subdominant can employ the scale of its tonic key (i.e. an FMA⁹ chord can use a C major scale because F is the subdominant chord in the key of C major). Additionally, a subdominant-functioning major chord can use the scale of its root (FMA⁹ - F Major scale). Example 4.7 depicts the IV (subdominant) MA⁷ harmony, with the two scale possibilities.

**Ex. 4.7  Two scales for sub-dominant harmony**

**Major 6(9) Chords** • A chord interchangeable with the major seventh is the major six-nine chord. The chords are similarly constructed, with a major sixth replacing the seventh of the chord, and they employ the same scales. The six-nine chord is typically used in the following situations:

1. as a substitute for major seventh.
2. alternating with major seventh in passages where one chord is in use for several measures.
3. as an alternative to major seventh, when the root is featured in the melody. A prominent root will tend to clash with a major seventh, but will be consonant against a sixth.

Example 4.8 shows the construction of a major six-nine chord.

**Ex. 4.8  Major six-nine chord**

## Consonance

The most consonant pitches to be emphasized with a major ninth chord are as follows:
1. the chord tones.
2. the sixth scale degree.
3. the raised fourth (lowered fifth) above the root.

The undesirable notes are:
1. a perfect fourth above the root.
2. the minor third.

3.  the minor seventh.
4.  one-half step above the root.

A major scale can be altered by raising the 4th degree a half step to be entirely consonant for major seventh harmony.  A review of Example 4.7 reveals that the primary scale for subdominant major seventh harmony *is* this scale with the raised 4th degree.  [Note: this is the *Lydian* scale from the diatonic "church" modes, as described in Chapter 22.]

**Beware the magnetic fourth and incorrect seventh!** • This study will reveal that most of the twelve tones seem to be consonant over any given chord.  This is not the case, however, with the note a perfect fourth above the root of a major chord, or a chromatically incorrect seventh over a major or dominant chord.  Even though it seems unlikely that an improviser would repeatedly stumble over these two notes, this is exactly what happens!  Therefore I conclude that these notes have a magnetic attraction to the new improviser and must be consciously fought in order to win the war of consonance.  Remember, if you play the fourth, you are only a half step away from the desirable third; and if you play the incorrect seventh, you can move by a half step into the correct seventh.  Good luck!

Example 4.9 illustrates the most consonant and least consonant notes above a major seventh chord, and melodies featuring each.  It should be obvious that the consonant melody is much more effective than the non-consonant one.

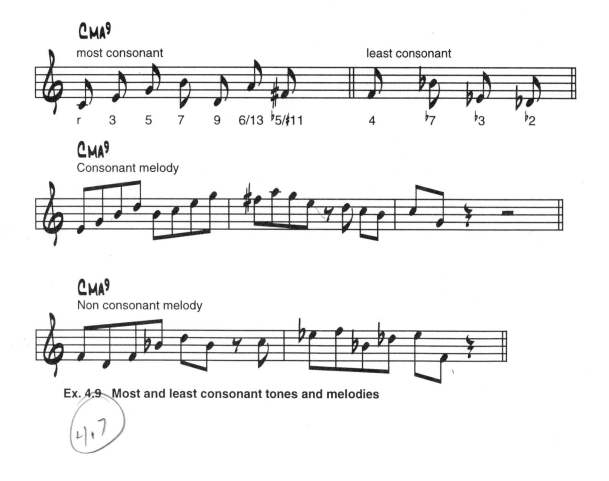

Ex. 4.9  Most and least consonant tones and melodies

**Formula: Grace Notes and Mordents** • One or several *grace notes* can be used to embellish a chord tone. Grace notes can also be used to connect chord tones. Example 4.10 demonstrates grace note usage.

**Ex. 4.10   Grace notes**

A *mordent* or turn is an embellishment which can connect two tones a step apart (see Example 4.11) or a third apart (see Example 4.12).

**Ex. 4.11   Mordents connecting a step or a 3rd apart (see Example 4.12)**

**Ex. 4.12   Mordents connecting a 3rd**

Example 4.13 shows the usage of mordents to embellish a scale.

**Ex. 4.13   Scale embellished by mordents**

Mordents can be indicated by the symbol ~ . Example 4.14 depicts the realization of the mordent symbol.

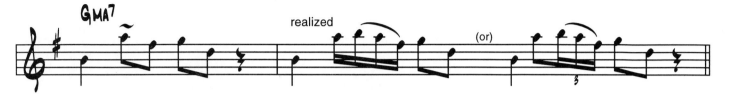

**Ex. 4.14   Realization of mordent symbol**

**Exercises**

1. Construct the following major seventh chords in root position and three inversions: GMA⁷, E♭MA⁷, AMA⁷, FMA⁷.

2. Construct the following major ninth chords in all four inversions (omitting the roots): G♭MA⁹, B♭MA⁹, DMA⁹, AMA⁹.

3. Notate the correct scales for the chords in Exercises 1 and 2, assuming both tonic and sub-dominant functions.

4. Add grace notes and mordents to the melodies below.

5. Practice the melodic figures from Examples 4.3 and 4.13 over the following chords: FMA⁷, GMA⁷, B♭MA⁷, and E♭MA⁷.

6. Prepare and employ a practice sheet for the tune *Majority* (see next page) using chord construction from 3rds to 9ths and the appropriate major scales. Play the practice sheet in class.

7. Compose a solo to *Majority*, emphasizing the goal-notes provided and employing characteristic melodic shape, grace notes and mordents. [Note: When goal notes are provided, the emphasis is on constructing *linear* ideas. Therefore, any goal note on a downbeat should continue a phrase from the preceding

measure.  The goal notes are placed strategically throughout the measures and effective notes should be placed in between.]

8.  Practice improvising to *Majority,* with lines passing through the goal notes provided.

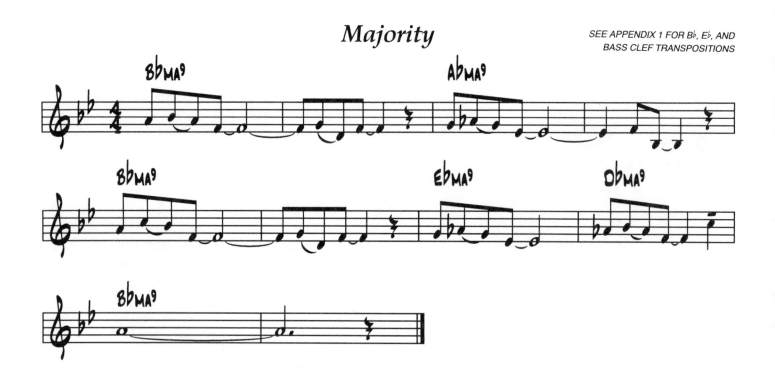

*Majority*

SEE APPENDIX 1 FOR B♭, E♭, AND BASS CLEF TRANSPOSITIONS

*Goal Notes for*
*Majority*

CHAPTER 5

# Dominant Seventh (Ninth) Chords
## X⁷, X⁹

## Construction

A dominant seventh chord is composed of a major triad with a minor seventh above the root.  It can be constructed by first building a major seventh chord and then lowering the chord-seventh chromatically (a half step).  The diatonic ninth is a major ninth above the root, although altered ninths are common (as discussed in Chapter 11).  The chord symbol for a dominant chord is simply to write the number 7 or 9 following the root name (i.e. $C^7$ or $C^9$).  Example 5.1 illustrates the notation of $C^7$ and $C^9$ chords.

**Ex. 5.1  Construction of dominant 7th and 9th chords**

## Function

Dominant seventh (9th) chords can have two different functions in jazz, as described below.

**Dominant Function** • Dominant chords are said to have a *dominant function*, which means that they precede a tonic chord in order to establish the key.  It should be noted that when a diatonic seventh chord is built on the fifth degree of any major scale (using that scale's major key signature), a dominant seventh chord always results.  Therefore, a dominant chord can function as a V chord in a key, and the progression V-I (Dominant-Tonic) establishes that key.  Virtually all classical compositions from Bach to Mahler employ the V-I progression to *cadence* (establish the key at phrase endings).  Example 5.2 depicts the construction of a dominant ($V^7$) chord in a major key.

**Ex. 5.2  Dominant 7th functions as $V^7$ in a key**

Example 5.3 demonstrates the progression V⁷-I (dominant-tonic) as it is used to estab-lish the key (cadence) in both classical and jazz music.

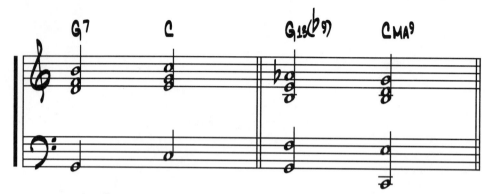

**Ex. 5.3  V⁷ - I; classical and jazz**

**"Bluesy" Sonorities** • In jazz music, dominant chords do not always convey dominant function.  Tunes are made to sound "bluesy" when dominant chords are used to replace non-dominant, diatonic chords.  So in a "bluesy" composition, C⁷ might be the I chord in the key of C.  The function of the dominant chord is determined by its place in the progression.  If the dominant chord is followed by another chord a perfect fifth down (or a perfect fourth up; i.e. G⁷-CMA⁷) at a point of resolution, then the chord is function-ing as a dominant.  But if the dominant chord seems to be establishing its own tonality, then it is being used as a "bluesy" sonority.  Example 5.4 depicts both functions of dom-inant harmony.

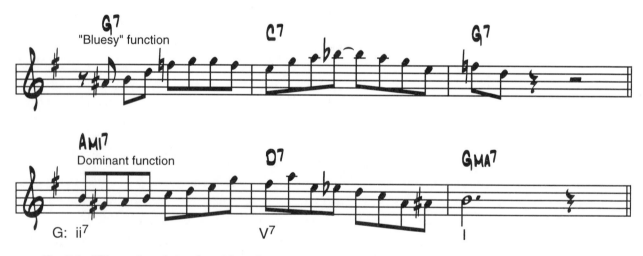

**Ex. 5.4  "Bluesy" and dominant functions**

**Resolution** • When a dominant 7th chord is used in a V-I progression, certain resolu-tions occur (a *resolution* takes place when the harmony leads a note to another note a step or half step away; the first note is said to *resolve* to the second note).  When V⁷ goes to I, the 7th and 9th of the dominant chord resolve down by step into the tonic chord. More specifically, the 7th of the dominant chord resolves to the 3rd of the tonic, and the

9th of the dominant resolves to the 5th of the tonic. It is very satisfying to the listener if the improviser effects a resolution as the chords change. Example 5.5 demonstrates the 7th and 9th resolutions in the progression $V^7$-I, as well as a characteristic jazz line employing these resolutions.

**Ex. 5.5   Resolutions: 7-3, 9-5**

**Term: Tendency Tones** • *Tendency tones* are the notes in a chord which require resolution.

**Term: Leading Tone** • The seventh note of a major scale is called *leading tone* because it leads to tonic. The 3rd of a dominant 7th chord (functioning as $V^7$) is leading tone.

In classical music, the 3rd of the dominant chord (leading tone) frequently resolves up to the root of the tonic chord. This resolution creates a "ti-do" sound. In jazz music, however, it is more likely for the 3rd of the dominant chord to remain stationary, in which case it becomes the 7th of the tonic chord. Example 5.6 shows the classical and jazz treatments of the 3rd of the dominant chord.

**Ex. 5.6   Classical and jazz treatments; 3rd of dominant chord**

**Scale** • The dominant seventh chord can be outlined by using a major scale with a lowered seventh scale degree (which can be referred to by its modal designation, Mixolydian). It should be understood, however, that the improviser is actually playing the major scale of the key in which that dominant chord functions. For instance, consider the chord $G^7$. If the G major scale is used with a lowered seventh degree (F♮), the scale that results is actually a C major scale, beginning and ending on G. This means that when an improviser plays a solo to the V-I progression $G^7$-$C_{MA}^7$, a C major scale is employed for both chords, and the improviser is said to be playing a cadence in C.

Example 5.7 displays the correct scale for a $C^{7(9)}$ chord. Notice that the C major scale with a lowered seventh is the same as F major, because $C^7$ is the dominant chord (V) in the key of F.

**Ex. 5.7   Scale for dominant harmony**

The above scale can be played with a raised fourth degree (as was the case for major seventh harmony) so that each note is a consonant tone.  This set of pitches, often called the Lydian dominant scale, is depicted in Example 5.8.

**Ex. 5.8   Lydian dominant scale**

## Consonance

The following rules apply to consonance over dominant seventh harmony:
1.  All scale tones, with the exception of the fourth above the root, are considered consonant and can be used at points of rest in the phrase.
2.  The only unacceptable notes for emphasis are the fourth and major seventh above the root.
3.  Many chromatic tones are also considered consonant, as will be discussed in Chapter 11.
4.  A raised fourth degree can replace the diatonic fourth to create consonance with all of the scale tones.

**Formula: Blue Notes and Blues Scale** • The *blue notes* are the chromatically lowered 3rd, 5th, and 7th notes of a key.  In the key of C Major these notes would be E♭, G♭, and B♭.  When used correctly these notes can create a "bluesy" sound with dominant chords built on I⁷, II⁷, IV⁷, V⁷, and in some instances VI⁷.  It is also possible to use the blue notes of individual chords by employing a minor 3rd, diminished 5th, and minor 7th over the chord root.  Example 5.9 demonstrates the blue notes of a key functioning over various chords.

**Ex. 5.9  Using "blues notes" with various chords**

5.8

The most efficient way to employ the blue notes is through the *blues scale.* The blues scale contains the scale degrees 1, ♭3, 4, ♭5, 5 and ♭7. Example 5.10 illustrates the C blues scale.

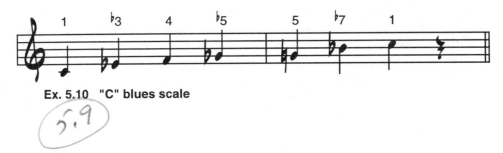

**Ex. 5.10  "C" blues scale**

5.9

The blues scale is most effectively used by creating licks in which the tones of the scale are played consecutively. For instance, ♭3 leads to 1 or 4; 4 leads to ♭3 or ♭5; ♭5 leads to 5 or 4; and ♭7 leads to 1 or ♭5. If the blue notes frequently skip out of sequence, the result is arpeggiation of an incorrect chord, and the bluesy effect is lost. Example 5.11 illustrates some characteristic blues scale licks.

**Ex. 5.11 Blues scale licks (G blues scale)**

5.10

Prolonged repetition of the blues scale will result in a monotonous solo. There is no law stating that the improviser cannot deviate from the notes of the blues scale; when Mozart wrote a piece in the key of C Major, he never limited himself to those seven notes! A welcome addition to any blue-note oriented lick or line is the inclusion of chord tones which may or may not be in the blues scale. Remember, the blues scale does not even contain the 3rd of the I chord, and this note is always desirable. Example 5.12 displays the usage of the blues scale with other chord tones.

**Ex. 5.12 Adding chord tones to the blues scale**

**Formula: Pentatonic/Blues Scale** • The *Pentatonic/Blues scale* is another effective combination of tones for lick-style playing. This scale is based upon the pentatonic scale, which is a major scale with tones 4 and 7 deleted. To the pentatonic scale a flatted 3rd is added, resulting in the tones 1, 2, ♭3, 3, 5, and 6 (efficient use of the pentatonic/blues scale is revealed in solos by David Sanborn and similar contemporary saxophone players). In its most typical usage, the pentatonic/blues scale highlights the relationships between 6 and ♭3, as well as ♭3 and 1. Example 5.13 shows the pentatonic/blues scale and its characteristic usage. [Note: a C pentatonic/blues scale contains the same tones as the A blues scale.]

**Ex. 5.13 "C" pentatonic/blues scale and usage**

**Term: Head** • The *head* is the original melody of a song. After all the solos have been played, the leader of the group instructs everyone to go back to the head, whereupon the tune is played for the final time.

## Exercises

1. Construct the following dominant 7th chords in root position and three inversions: $E^7$, $B♭^7$, $G^7$, $C♯^7$.

2. Construct the following dominant 9th chords in all four inversions (omitting the roots): $E♭^9$, $B^9$, $A♭^9$, $F^9$.

3. Notate the correct scales for the chords in Exercises 1 and 2.

4. Construct blues scales and pentatonic/blues scales in the following major keys: C, F, G, B♭, and E.

5. Compose licks to several dominant chords, employing blues scales and pentatonic/blues scales.

6. Prepare and employ a practice sheet for the tune *Dominant Functions*, using chord construction from 3rds to 9ths, and the appropriate scales.

7. Compose a solo to *Dominant Functions*, emphasizing the goal notes provided and employing characteristic melodic shape, grace notes and mordents, blues scales, and/or pentatonic/blues scales.

8. Identify and practice all tendency tone resolutions found within the tune *Dominant Functions*.

9. Practice improvising to the progression of *Dominant Functions*, allowing lines to pass through the goal notes provided.

10. Analyze the sample solo to *Dominant Functions* (Appendix 2), identifying characteristic jazz formulae, tendency tone resolution, and the usage of blues scales and licks.

# Dominant Functions

SEE APPENDIX 1 FOR B♭, E♭, AND BASS CLEF TRANSPOSITIONS

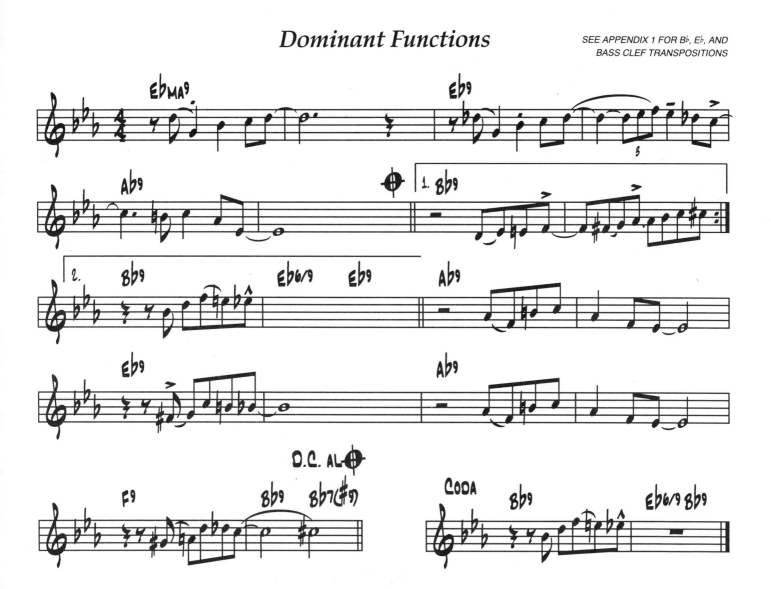

*Goal Notes for*
## Dominant Functions

CHAPTER 6

# Minor Seventh (Ninth) Chords
## X$\text{MI}^7$

variant symbols: X$\text{min}^9$, X$\text{m}^9$, X$^{-9}$

## Construction

A minor seventh chord is composed of a minor triad, with a minor seventh above the root. A minor triad can be constructed by beginning with a major triad, then lowering the 3rd of the chord chromatically (a half step). So a minor seventh chord can be built by beginning with the major seventh chord, and then lowering both the 3rd and 7th of the chord a half step. The ninth is always a major ninth above the root. Example 6.1 displays the C$\text{MI}^7$ and C$\text{MI}^9$ chords.

Ex. 6.1  C$\text{MI}^7$ and C$\text{MI}^9$ chords

## Function

**ii-Chord (Supertonic) Function** • When seventh chords are built on the second, third and sixth scale degrees of any major key, using that key signature, minor seventh chords (MI$^7$) always result. By far, the most prevalently used minor seventh chord is the one constructed over the second scale degree. This chord is said to have a ii-chord or *supertonic* function. Example 6.2 displays the C major scale and the D$\text{MI}^7$ chord which functions as supertonic, as well as the diatonic minor seventh chords resulting over the third and sixth degrees.

Ex. 6.2  D$\text{MI}^7$ as diatonic ii$^7$ chord

[Note: in the case of major or dominant chords, capital Roman numerals are employed. Minor triads are indicated by lower-case Roman numerals.]

In jazz music, the ii⁷ chord progresses to V⁷ with great regularity. For instance, in the key of C major, the ii⁷ chord (DMI⁷) will often be followed by the V⁷ chord (G⁷).

**Resolution** • When ii⁷ progresses to V⁷, the root motion is up a perfect fourth (or down a perfect fifth). This is exactly the same relationship as when V⁷ progresses to I. The progression is ii⁷-V⁷-I moves entirely in descending fifths, creating a progression from the *circle of fifths* (see Appendix 3). Because of the circle of fifths, the same resolving tendencies apply to the progression ii⁷-V⁷ that were observed in the progression V⁷-I. This means that the seventh of the ii chord resolves down to the third of the V, the ninth resolves down to the fifth, and the third remains stationary to become the seventh. Example 6.3 depicts the resolution of chord tones in the progression ii⁹-V⁹, and a charactertistic jazz line employing proper resolution.

**Ex. 6.3   Resolutions: ii⁷-V⁷**

**Scale** • When a minor seventh chord is functioning as ii⁷, the proper scale is the major scale of the key in which the chord functions. In other words, when DMI⁷is functioning as ii⁷ in C major, a C major scale is employed, beginning and ending on D. This mode of the major scale, beginning on the second degree, is referred to as *Dorian*. This means that the progression DMI⁷-G⁷-CMA⁷ can be improvised based entirely on the notes of the C major scale because all three chords function diatonically in C (ii⁷-V⁷-I⁷). [Obviously it is desirable to employ chromatic pitches around the chord tones as well, irrespective of the preferred scale.] Example 6.4 shows the E♭ major scale from F to F as it is used for an FMI⁹ chord functioning as ii⁹.

**Ex. 6.4   FMI⁹ chord and scale (E♭ major)**

**iii⁷ and vi⁷ (mediant and submediant) Function** • As mentioned above, for any major key, chords built on the third and sixth scale degrees will also be minor seventh chords. While these chords do occur occasionally, they are often replaced with dominant chords (as discussed in subsequent chapters). A minor iii⁷ or vi⁷ can be determined by the surrounding progression and the eventual V⁷-I in the expected key. Example 6.5 depicts the iii⁷ and vi⁷ chords in B♭ major. [Note: a diatonic iii⁹ chord might not contain a ninth, as this note is chromatic to the key.]

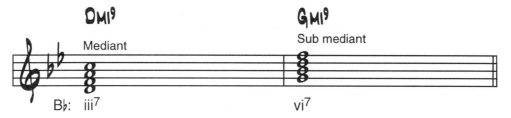

Ex. 6.5  iii⁷ and vi⁷ in B♭ major

In the circle of fifths (Appendix 3), iii⁷ progresses to vi⁷, which progresses to ii⁷ and so on. While these chords are not bound or required to move in the circle of fifths, this is often the case. Example 6.6 displays a jazz melody over the circle of fifths progression employing iii⁷ and vi⁷.

Ex. 6.6  **Jazz melody to circle of fifth proression (iii⁷-vi⁷-ii⁷-V⁷-I)**

**Scale** • When a minor seventh chord is functioning as iii⁷ or vi⁷, the scale of the key in which the chord functions is preferable. Therefore, in the key of C major, an improvised melody to both EMI⁷ and AMI⁷ can be based upon the C major scale.

## Consonance

The following rules of consonance apply to minor seventh chords:
1. When a minor seventh chord functions as ii⁹, all scale tones are consonant and can be used at points of rest.
2. The perfect fourth above the root is a consonant tone and is considered to be an 11th extension to the harmony.
3. When using the minor seventh as a iii⁷ or vi⁷, the fourth note of the key is not consonant (i.e. when EMI⁷ and AMI⁷ function in C major, F is not a consonant

tone).

4. The non-consonant tones above a minor seventh chord are the major third, major seventh, half step above the root, and a tritone above the root.

**Formula: Combined Scale/Arpeggio** • One way to ensure that scales are used in a consonant manner is to skip from one chord to the next, creating *combined scale/arpeggios*. There are many possible ways to construct combined scale/arpeggios, far too numerous to explore here. Example 6.7 depicts some sample scale/arpeggio figures which can be practiced in all keys and with all chord types.

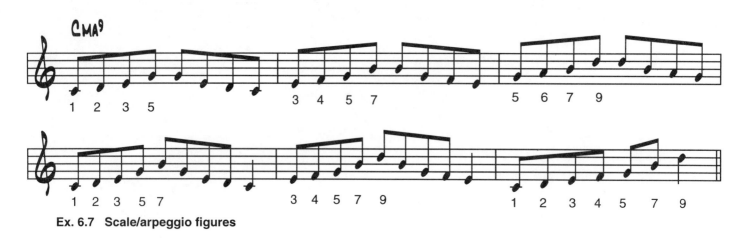

Ex. 6.7  Scale/arpeggio figures

**Formula: Sequence** • A melodic *sequence* is the repetition of a musical idea at different pitch levels. The usage of sequence can be a unifying device to an improvised solo. Example 6.8 illustrates a jazz melody including melodic sequence.

Ex. 6.8  Melody with sequence

**Term: Chorus** • A *chorus* is an improvised solo one time through the progression (changes) of a song.

### Exercises

1. Construct the following minor seventh chords in root position and three inversions: AMI⁷, B♭MI⁷, CMI⁷, EMI⁷.
2. Construct the following minor ninth chords in all four inversions (omitting the roots): G♯MI⁹, D♭MI⁹, FMI⁹, BMI⁹.
3. Notate the correct scales for the chords in Exercises 1 and 2.
4. Practice the scale/arpeggio figures from Example 6.7 for major 7th and minor 7th chords over the following roots: C, F, G, B♭, E♭, D, A♭.
5. Prepare and employ a practice sheet for the tune *Minor Difficulties*, using chord construction from 3rds to 9ths, and the appropriate scales.
6. Compose a solo to *Minor Difficulties* emphasizing the goal notes provided, and employing sequence, characteristic melodic shape and applicable jazz formulae. Be sure to analyze the goal notes (Which notes of the chords are used? Do resolutions occur?).
7. Analyze the sample solo to *Minor Difficulties* (Appendix 2), identifying characteristic jazz formulae, tendency tone resolutions, combined scale/arpeggio and melodic sequence.
8. Practice improvising to the progression of *Minor Difficulties*, allowing lines to pass through the goal notes provided, or alternately effecting tendency tone resolutions.

## *Minor Difficulties*

SEE APPENDIX 1 FOR B♭, E♭, AND
BASS CLEF TRANSPOSITIONS

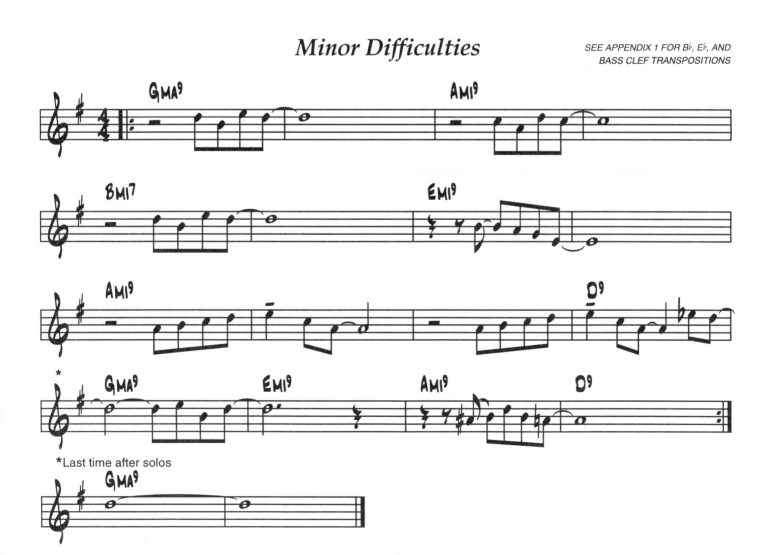

*Last time after solos

*Goal Notes for*
## Minor Difficulties

CHAPTER 7

# The 12-Bar Blues

## Form

The 12-bar blues progression is the most-recorded and most-performed song form in jazz. Although there are many possible permutations to the progression (see Chapter 19), all 12-bar blues forms share similar aspects and harmonic goals. The original blues progression (used more frequently by blues performers than jazz artists) was based on three chords. Example 7.1 depicts this basic 12-bar blues progression.

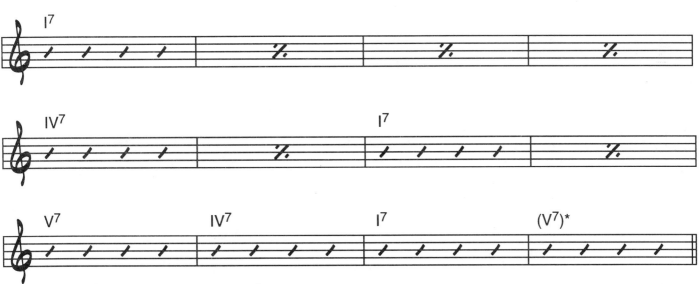

**Ex. 7.1  Basic 12 bar blues progression**

[* - Parenthetical chords are optional. In this case, the chord in parenthesis helps return the progression to tonic for the next chorus, so it would be played every time except the last.]

Originally the 12-bar blues was organized in a *call and response* fashion. In "call and response," a musical (and lyric) idea is introduced in the first four bars, answered (repeated) in the second four bars, and concludes with a new idea in the last four bars. In the melody and lyric, measures 1-8 seem to pose a question or problem, while the last phrase provides the solution or resolution. *Little "J" Blues* at the end of this chapter is organized in the "call and response" form.

The 12-bar blues contains three harmonic ideas:
1. measures 1-4 establish the key.
2. measures 5-8 begin on the IV chord and return towards tonic.
3. measures 9-12 reestablish the tonic through cadence.

*Little "J" Blues* (page 40) provides an example of a basic *jazz blues* progression, in which a jazz cadence (ii⁷-V⁷-I) is added to reestablish tonic at the end of the form. The jazz blues progression also uses a IV chord in the second measure. [Note: The head of a 12-bar blues song is normally played twice before the solos begin.]

## Improvisation

Some key factors concerning improvisation to a 12-bar blues progression are as follows:

1.  Both the blues scale and pentatonic/blues scale are effective over all the chords of the progression, although a prolonged solo over a single blues scale is not typical to jazz performance.
2.  Going from measure 1 to 2 of the jazz blues (I⁷-IV⁷) allows for the 3rd of the I chord to be lowered a half step, thus becoming the 7th of the IV chord in m. 2. For example, in *Little "J" Blues*, the 3rd of the I chord (C⁷) is E♮, which can move in measure 2 to E♭, the 7th of the IV chord (F⁷). There are three opportunities to execute this *3rd to 7th interchange* during the 12-bar blues: mm. 1-2, 2-3, 6-7 (see Example 7.3).
3.  It is important to emphasize the 7th of the I⁷ in m. 4. In the circle of fifths, I⁷ progresses to IV (up a perfect 4th), therefore, the 7th of the I⁷ can resolve to the 3rd of the IV⁷ as measure 4 changes to m. 5. In *Little "J" Blues*, Bb is the 7th of the I⁷ (C⁷) and it resolves to A, the third of IV⁷ (F⁷); see Examples 7.2 and 7.4.
4.  A good place to abandon the blues-scale style of playing is mm. 9-10, where the ii⁷-V⁷ chord structure is more progressive sounding.

Example 7.2 shows some appropriate goal notes for the jazz blues progression, based on the factors outlined above.

**Ex. 7.2   Goal notes for "Little J Blues"**

Example 7.3 shows the effective usage of a lick to accentuate the chromatic relationship between the 3rd of the I⁷ chord and the 7th of the IV⁷ chord (3rd to 7th interchange).

**Ex. 7.3   Lick employing chromatic alteration (mm. 1-3)**

Example 7.4 demonstrates the emphasis of the 7th of the I⁷ chord in measure 4, and then the resolution to the 3rd of the IV⁷ chord in measure 5.

**Ex. 7.4   Emphasizing and resolving the 7th (mm. 4-5)**

[Note: The sample solo in Appendix 2 demonstrates the factors of improvisation described above.]

**Formula: Chromatic Passing to Dominant 7th** • It is common for jazz improvisers to construct lines which pass chromatically from the root to the 7th of a dominant chord. Employing this technique will emphasize the 7th of I⁷ in the fourth bar of the blues progression. Example 7.5 shows the typical usage of chromatic passing to 7th in bar 4 of a 12-bar blues.

**Ex. 7.5   Chromatic passing to chord 7th**

**Scale: Be-bop Dominant** • A scale which highlights the chromatic passing to 7th is often called the *be-bop dominant scale.* This is simply a major scale, usually played in descending order, in which the minor seventh and major seventh tones are both used. The advantageous characteristic of be-bop dominant scale is that it places all four chord tones, from root to 7th, on the beats, even when played for more than one octave. This scale is used with great regularity by jazz players. Example 7.6 displays construction of the be-bop dominant scale.

**Ex. 7.6   Be-Bop dominant scale**

**Formula: Triplet Arpeggio** • A common melodic cell for jazz improvisation is the triplet arpeggio. The *triplet arpeggio* usually begins off the beat a half-step below the root or 3rd of a chord, and arpeggiates up the chord tones in a triplet rhythm. Example 7.7 illustrates the most frequently-played triplet arpeggios, from the root and 3rd of the chord.

**Ex. 7.7   Triplet arpeggio figures**

The triplet arpeggio is a very versatile figure, and as such can be used almost anywhere in the phrase. It is also seen in descending form, although in this context it usually begins right on a chord tone. Example 7.8 shows a jazz melody employing triplet arpeggios.

**Ex. 7.8   Using triplet arpeggios**

**Formula: Using Licks in 12-Bar Blues** • There are two basic concepts for using licks in a 12-bar blues. First of all, a lick can be constructed using one of the blues scales and can be repeated as the chord change. Example 7.9 depicts a lick over which the blues progression can be played.

**Ex. 7.9   Sample lick for blues**

It is also possible to construct licks in which one or more notes will change with the chords. As mentioned above, a lick containing the 3rd of the I$^7$ chord might require only that note to change (down a half step) as it progresses to the IV$^7$ chord (Example 7.3). Example 7.10 displays a lick which changes with the chords.

**Ex. 7.10   Lick with alterations**

It is also possible to completely transpose licks as the chords change, or simply to vary the licks to avoid monotony and achieve growth. In any song, it is appropriate to begin a chorus with a memorable lick which develops into more linear ideas as the solo chorus progresses (see Example 7.11).

**Ex. 7.11   Developing from a lick**

**Exercises**

1. Prepare and employ a practice sheet for the tune *Little "J" Blues* using chord construction from 3rds to 9ths, and the appropriate scales.
2. Notate and practice the be-bop dominant scales for *Little "J" Blues*.
3. Compose several licks for *Little "J" Blues*, and practice alterations and variations to fit the structure and changes.
4. Practice triplet arpeggios to *Little "J" Blues*.

5. Compose a solo to *Little "J" Blues* employing goal notes, characteristic melodic shape, and applicable jazz formula.

6. Analyze and/or transcribe recorded blues solos brought in by students or the instructor. Listen for resolutions, triplet arpeggios, chromatic passing, licks, and other applicable idioms.

7. Analyze the sample solo to *Little "J" Blues* (Appendix 2), identifying characteristic jazz formulae, including those discussed in this chapter.

## *Little "J" Blues*

SEE APPENDIX 1 FOR B♭, E♭, AND
BASS CLEF TRANSPOSITIONS

CHAPTER 8

# Auxiliary Tones and Chromaticism

This study of jazz improvisation has thus far centered around the usage of chord tones and scales. It is important to understand that a mature style of improvisation requires the development of a chromatic style in which all twelve tones are employed liberally. This concept can be advanced greatly through an understanding of auxiliary tones and chromatic passing tones in the jazz concept.

## Auxiliary Tones

*Auxiliary tones* are the notes within one step of a chord tone in either direction. In classical music, an auxiliary tone will most often lead directly to the chord tone it embellishes. In jazz improvisation, however, several auxiliary tones can be played consecutively prior to the line coming to a rest on a chord tone. Example 8.1 demonstrates the use of auxiliary tones to embellish notes of the chord.

**Ex. 8.1  Auxiliary tones**

The pertinent facts concerning auxiliary tones are as follows:
1. The most prevalently used auxiliaries are the note a half step *below* a chord tone, the note a half step *above* a chord tone, and the note a whole step *above* a chord tone.
2. The note a whole step below a chord tone is not always effective and often must pass through the note a half step below on its way back to the chord tone.
3. Auxiliary tones are normally used surrounding the roots, 3rds, and 5ths of chords. At times 6ths and 7ths are embellished, but rarely are auxiliary tones used around extensions beyond the 7th, as the harmony can become ambigious.
4. The note a whole step above the 7th of a major seventh chord is not a consonant auxiliary.
5. Auxiliary tones can be used to anticipate a chord change or after a chord has changed. They can occur on the beat or off.
6. Multiple auxiliary tones are used with great frequency in jazz improvisation, to the extent that phrases can be constructed entirely of chord tones and auxiliaries.

Example 8.2 designates the auxiliary tones around the notes of the CMA⁷ chord.

**Ex. 8.2 Auxiliary tones to CMA⁷**

Example 8.3 provides characteristic auxiliary motives which should be practiced in all keys and around all the basic chord tones.

**Ex. 8.3 Auxiliary figures around a chord root**

Example 8.4 shows a melody constructed entirely of chord tones and auxiliary tones.

**Ex. 8.4 Melody of chord tones and auxiliaries**

A tendency tone in the circle of fifths is a half step higher than the note of resolution, and can be combined with a note below the resolving tone to create auxiliary tone figures (see Example 8.5).

**Ex. 8.5 Combining auxiliary tones with resolution**

## Chromatic Passing Tones

The main requirements to "playing the changes" are establishing the chord tones, effecting resolutions in the circle of fifths, and respecting the heirarchy of consonant tones (liberal 3rd and 7th emphasis).  When these tasks have been completed, the melodic line makes sense and carefully placed chromatic tones will not obscure the harmony, but rather make the line sound more interesting and varied.  In classical music these chromatic tones are referred to as *decorative chromaticism.*  There are a few ways to use chromatic passing tones effectively.
1.  The principle chord tones should appear on the beats frequently enough to keep the harmony clear.
2.  Syncopation can be used to allow the line to stop on a chord tone.  This can be achieved by arriving at the chord tone on an upbeat, and leaving the chord tone on the next upbeat.
3.  It is a common melodic formula to begin a melody one step above or below a chord tone and pass chromatically to it.  This device can also occur after a skip from another chord tone.
4.  Each principle chord tone can be preceded by its leading tone (the note a half step below or above the chord tone).

Example 8.6 shows the *leading tones* between the chord tones of major 7th harmony.

**Ex. 8.6  Leading tones (upper and lower) to chord tones**

Example 8.7 displays chromatic passing, emphasizing syncopation and the leading tones to chord members.

**Ex. 8.7  Chromatic passing: syncopation and secondary leading tones**

Example 8.8 demonstrates chromatic passing from one step above and below chord tones.

**Ex. 8.8   Chromatic passing from a step above**

Be-bop scales can be constructed for major 7th and minor 7th harmony using chromatic passing; see Example 8.9.

**Ex. 8.9   Be-Bop scales for major 7th and minor 7th harmony**

The use of passing chromaticism in scalar passages effectively places consonant tones on more of the beats, as depicted in Example 8.10.

**Ex. 8.10   Using chromaticism places consonance on the beats**

When used in combination with previously described principles and formulae, the types of chromaticism outlined in this chapter can greatly enhance the maturity and variety of the improviser's style.  Example 8.11 depicts the combination of auxiliary and other decorative chromaticism in the jazz melodic line.

**Ex. 8.11   Jazz melody with decorative chromaticism**

**Exercises**

1. Compose 4-bar melodies, employing only auxiliary tones and chord tones, to the following chords: FMA$^9$, EMI$^9$, B$\flat$$^9$, DMI$^9$, and E$\flat$$^9$.

2. Compose 4-bar melodies, employing auxiliaries and chromatic passing tones, to the following chords: GMA$^9$, CMI$^9$, A$^9$, D$^9$, and A$\flat$MA$^9$.

3. Analyze transcribed solos brought in by students or instructor, paying particular attention to chromatic passing tones and auxiliaries. Also look for triplet arpeggio, combined scale/arpeggio, resolutions, characteristic phrasing and rhythms.

4. Prepare and employ a practice sheet to the tune *Mellotones*.

5. Compose a solo to *Mellotones* using goal notes and the types of decorative chromaticism described in this chapter.

6. Practice be-bop scales for major 7th and minor 7th harmony in all keys.

7. Practice the leading tone figure of Example 8.7 in all keys.

8. Over one chord at a time, practice extended 8th-note lines (4-10 measures) consisting predominantly of chord tones and decorative chromaticism.

9. Practice improvising to *Mellotones*, emphasizing auxiliary tones, chromatic passing, and tendency tone resolution.

10. Analyze the sample solo to *Mellotones* (Appendix 2), identifying characteristic jazz formulae, including decorative chromaticism.

## Mellotones

*SEE APPENDIX 1 FOR B$\flat$, E$\flat$, AND BASS CLEF TRANSPOSITIONS*

CHAPTER 9

# Turnaround Progression
## ii⁷-V⁷-Iᴍᴀ⁷

The diatonic progression of ii⁷-V⁷-Iᴍᴀ⁷ is used to establish keys and create cadences in jazz. This progression is called a *turnaround*. The important facts concerning turnarounds are as follows.

1. This is a circle-of-fifths progression and implies tendency tone resolutions.
2. Turnaround progressions typically make up about 75% of the harmony of jazz standards. Therefore, an improviser who is proficient with turnarounds has grasped the greater part of the art which is jazz improvisation!
3. The harmony in most jazz standards can be seen as a series of turnaround progressions, establishing various keys, and concluding with a return to tonic (indicated by a cadence in the original key).
4. Jazz tunes often present various ii-V progressions which do not resolve to their I chords. As a result, learning the play the ii-V progression is the most crucial element in mastering turnarounds.

## Improvisation

The essence of turnaround playing can be summed up with the following rules and procedures:

1. The circle-of-fifth resolutions (7-3, 9-5, 3 becomes 7) are usually expected when ii progresses to V, and are often employed for V-I (especially 7th resolving to 3rd).
2. These resolutions can occur one or two beats before or after the chords change. Neither the expectation nor the satisfaction of the resolutions are diminished by the unexpected rhythmic placement.
3. Turnaround lines are often initiated with auxiliary figures to the root or third of the ii chord. Combined scale/arpeggio frequently follows.
4. Chromatic passing from root to seventh of the dominant chord, as well as the be-bop dominant scale are both prominent formulae to turnaround lines.
5. Licks are used less frequently in turnaround progressions, but all other aspects of jazz melody and phrasing are important to consider and include when constructing melodic lines.

Example 9.1 displays turnaround lines with 7th to 3rd resolutions occurring at various times within the progression.

**Ex. 9.1   7th to 3rd resolution at various metric points**

Example 9.2 demonstrates the usage of auxiliaries to initiate turnaround lines, and the practice of chromatic passing to the 7th of the dominant chord.

**Ex. 9.2   Auxiliary and chromatic passing to 7th**

**Formula: the Combined Scale/Arpeggio Turnaround Line** • The previously described techniques of combined scale/arpeggio and tendency tone (7th to 3rd) resolution can be juxtaposed to create a typical ii-V melodic formula, the *combined scale/arpeggio turnaround line*, depicted in Example 9.3.

**Ex. 9.3   The combined scale/arpeggio turnaround line**

Appendix 6 begins with ten turnaround lines which are variations of the combined scale/arpeggio turnaround line.

**One-Measure ii-V Turnarounds** • It is typical for ii-V progressions to occur within one measure, where each chord lasts two beats. In these instances, certain formula-based motives can be employed to create lines. For harmonic clarity, these motives contain both the 3rd and 7th of each chord, followed by tendency tone resolution. Example 9.4 depicts the motives, which are constructed from the following tones above the chord root: 3-4-5-7, 3-5-R-7, and 3-2-1-7. Each of these four-note groupings forms a cell (or module) which can be interchanged with the others to create a variety of melodies.

**Ex. 9.4   Formulae for one measure turnarounds**

Example 9.5 shows how arpeggiation can be a melodic source for one-measure turn-arounds.

**Ex. 9.5   Arpeggiation for one measure turnarounds**

**Formula: Passing Minor ♯7** • As indicated above, the seventh of the ii chord regularly resolves to the third of the V chord. By employing arpeggiation, and passing chromatically to the seventh prior to resolution, the improviser can create another type of formula-based turnaround line. Prior to playing the minor 7th of the chord, the improviser actually passes through a minor ♯7 chord (that is, a minor triad with a major 7th above the root). Example 9.6 demonstrates the chromatic passing through MI♯7 harmony in turnaround lines (see Appendix 6 for more examples).

**Ex. 9.6  Passing MI♯7 chord**

**Term: 32-Bar (Standard) Song Form** • Many standard jazz tunes are in the *standard* or *32-bar song form*. The standard form consists of four 8-measure phrases. The first, second, and fourth phrases are almost identical, with differing first and second endings, while the third phrase is contrasting. The resultant form can be described as AABA, with the "B" section being called the *bridge* (some old-timers call it the *channel* or the *release*). Standard songs such as *Misty, As Time Goes By, Take The "A" Train*, and *Satin Doll* are all in the 32-bar standard form.

There are a few inherent difficulties in playing standard songs. They are as follows:

1. There are three opportunities to play "A" each chorus, and only one chance to try "B". Therefore, it is not uncommon for an improviser to be unprepared with the chord changes of the bridge.
2. Sometimes the bridge is forgotten entirely, and the players are forced to make something up in order to save face. It is not a bad idea to devote extra practice time to the bridge when learning a new song.
3. Players often confuse the form of standard songs. In a chorus, after the bridge has been played, an "A" section follows. The next chorus begins with two more "A" sections. Improvisers often omit the last "A", thinking that it is time for the bridge. It must be remembered that between bridges there are three "A" sections, as illustrated by the diagram below.

## AABA  AABA

**Diagram 9.1  Two choruses of standard song form**

It should be noted that an almost equal number of 32-bar standard songs are constructed in a "bridgeless" form, consisting of two 16-bar halves. These songs can be arranged in ABAB, ABAC, or variations of these two forms. *Just Friends, My Romance, The Days Of Wine and Roses*, and *There Will Never Be Another You* are all examples of the *bridgeless* standard song form.

**Exercises**

1. Construct turnaround lines in the major keys of C, F, G, B♭, E♭, and A♭, making each chord one bar long. Be sure to employ the formulae described above.
2. Construct turnaround lines in the above keys, where the ii and V chords are two beats long and the I chord encompasses the second measure.
3. Prepare and employ a practice sheet for the tune on the next page, *Catch A Caboose*.
4. Prepare a solo to *Catch A Caboose*. Compose certain ii-V lines, but improvise the remainder of the solo.
5. Listen to and discuss standard songs on recordings. Listen for turnaround progressions and whether or not tunes are in the standard form.
6. Practice the combined scale/arpeggio turnaround line in all keys.
7. Practice one-bar turnaround lines employing the four-note groupings in all keys.

8.  Analyze the sample solo to *Catch A Caboose* (Appendix 2), identifying characteristic jazz formulae and specific turnaround devices.

# Catch A Caboose

SEE APPENDIX 1 FOR B♭, E♭, AND
BASS CLEF TRANSPOSITIONS

# SECTION 3

# Chromatic Harmony

CHAPTER 10

# Turnaround to IV

Other than the turnaround to I (cadence) that must occur in every standard song, the next most prevalent tonicisation in jazz is the turnaround to the IV chord. Tunes like *I've Got Rhythm, There Will Never Be Another You, Misty, Satin Doll, Take The "A" Train, Just Friends,* and countless others all feature this progression.

In that IV⁷ is a major 7th chord in every major key, it can be made to sound like a new tonic simply by preceding it with the appropriate ii and V.

Here are the facts concerning turnarounds to the IV chord:
1. Because I is a perfect fourth below IV, a dominant seventh chord built on I *is* the dominant of IV. For instance, in the key of C major, Cᴍᴀ⁷ is I and Fᴍᴀ⁷ is IV; but in the key of F major, C⁷ is V and Fᴍᴀ⁷ is I. Therefore, by turning I into a dominant chord (Cᴍᴀ⁷ becomes C⁷) and progressing to IV, the improviser has affected a turnaround to IV (and IV sounds like a new tonic).

Example 10.1 shows the relationship of C-F as I-IV and V-I.

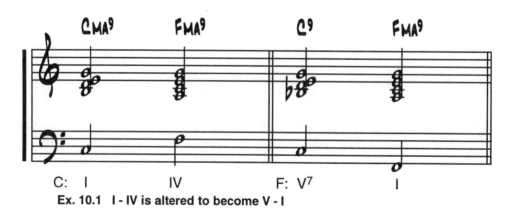

Ex. 10.1   I - IV is altered to become V - I

2. A complete turnaround to IV is created by preceding it with its ii chord and its V. In every key, a minor 7th chord built on V will function as the ii⁷ chord to IV. In C major, Gᴍɪ⁷-C⁷-Fᴍᴀ⁷ affects the complete turnaround to IV (notice that this is exactly the same as ii⁷-V⁷-I in F major).

Example 10.2 displays the complete turnaround to IV.

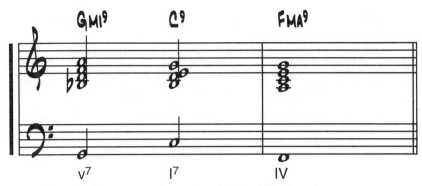

Ex. 10.2 Turnaround progression to IV in C major

## Improvisation

In order to effect the turnaround to IV, the improviser changes the I chord from a major 7th to a dominant 7th simply by lowering the 7th of the I chord a half step. It is this lowered seventh of the I[7] that clarifies and defines the turnaround to IV. Therefore, it is the obligation of the player to emphasize the *lowered seventh scale degree* at the beginning of any turnaround to IV. [Note: lowered 7th scale degree is also present in the ii[7] chord of this progression (vMI[7]). It is the third of this chord.] Example 10.3 demonstrates a jazz melody which emphasizes lowered seventh scale degree in the turnaround progression to IV.

Ex. 10.3  Emphasizing lowered 7th scale degree

**Formula: Chromatic Passing** • As stated above, the lowered seventh scale degree is the operable note in defining a turnaround progression to the IV chord. As a result, the formula of passing chromatically from root to seventh of a dominant chord is most effective in emphasizing this note, as depicted in Example 10.4. [Note: these same tones also connect 4th to 3rd over the corresponding ii chord, which is likewise displayed in Example 10.4.]

**Ex. 10.4   Chromatic passing to 7th of dominant (3rd of ii)**

A turnaround to the IV chord is actually the same as any other ii⁷-V⁷-I progression, but it is helpful to remember that the lowered seventh scale degree is the facilitating note of the progression. After all, when comparing two keys a perfect fourth apart, it is noticed that they share all of the same pitches except for one. The lowered seventh scale degree of the original tonic is the note which modulates the song to the new key up a perfect fourth (i.e. B♭ is the one note which differentiates the keys of C major and F major).

**Formula: Smooth Arpeggiation ii⁹-V¹³** • When practicing the arpeggios of a ii-V progression it is useful for the player to emphasize the resolution from 7th to 3rd. This emphasis can be achieved by placing the V chord in inversion. The process is as follows:

1. Play the ii⁹ chord from 3rd to 9th.
2. Play the chord again, resolving the 7th down by a half step but leaving the other notes as they are.
3. The resulting chord is a V⁷ chord, which contains a 13th instead of a fifth (a 13th is a 6th in a chord which also contains a 7th). This new chord is called V¹³.

Example 10.5 demonstrates the use of inversions to arpeggiate smoothly from ii⁹-V¹³. Notice that only one note is required to change between the two chords.

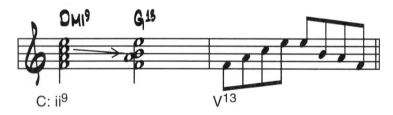

**Ex. 10.5   Smooth arpeggiation: ii⁹ - V¹³**

It should be noted that the 13th above a dominant chord is another tendency tone which will resolve downward to the 9th of the tonic, as seen in Example 10.6.

**Ex. 10.6   13 to 9 resolution**

**Exercises**

1. Construct turnaround melodies to the IV chord in the following major keys: C, Eb, D, F, and Ab. Begin with two measures of IMA$^7$, followed by a bar each of vMI$^7$, I$^7$ and IVMA$^7$.
2. Notate chords for practice arpeggiation of the ii$^9$-V$^{13}$-IMA$^9$ progression in the following major keys: G, Bb, Eb, and F. Only one note should change between ii$^9$ and V$^{13}$.
3. Review other songs in this book and identify turnarounds to the IV chord.
4. Analyze transcribed solos and recordings, paying particular attention to lines which cadence on IV.
5. Prepare and employ a practice sheet for the tune *Lacey Lady*, utilizing the principle of smooth arpeggiation from ii-V.
6. Compose a solo to *Lacey Lady*, emphasizing goal notes, resolution, chromatic passing, and a clear turnaround to the IV chord.
7. Analyze the sample solo to *Lacey Lady* (Appendix 2), identifying characteristic jazz formulae, turnaround lines, and the turnaround to IV.

## Lacey Lady

SEE APPENDIX 1 FOR Bb, Eb, AND
BASS CLEF TRANSPOSITIONS

CHAPTER 11

# Turnarounds to Minor Tonics
## $X_{MI}{}^{\sharp 7}$, $X_{MI}{}^{6(9)}$, $ii^{\varnothing 7}$
### Altered Dominant Ninths
### The Turnback Progression

## Tonic Minor

Just as there are classical compositions based around minor tonics, it is possible for jazz songs to turnaround to minor keys. The pertinent facts about minor tonics are:

1. Minor seventh chords do not make effective tonics because they tend to sound like $ii^7$ chords in a jazz context.

2. Minor triads with raised 7ths ($MI^{\sharp 7}$) and minor six/nine chords are the suitable minor tonics. These chords can be seen as derivative of the ascending melodic minor scale.

3. Alterations are necessary to ii and V chords when establishing a turnaround to a minor chord.

4. Bluesy melodies can be effective over minor tonics and turnarounds.

**Minor #7 Chord ($MI^{\sharp 7}$)** • The *minor ♯7 chord* is a minor triad with a major 7th above the root. It is considered consonant and can be used as a tonic at points of rest in the progression. The ninth is a major ninth above the root. Example 11.1 depicts the $MI^{\sharp 7}$ and $MI^{9(\sharp 7)}$ chords.

Ex. 11.1  $MI^{+7}$ and $MI^{9+7}$ chords

**Minor 6(9) Chord** • The *minor six/nine chord* is interchangeable with the minor ♯7, and is likewise based on ascending melodic minor scale. This chord contains a minor triad with a major sixth and major ninth above the root. Example 11.2 displays the minor 6(9) chord.

Ex. 11.2   minor six/nine chord

**Scale** • Minor tonics employ an ascending melodic minor scale in both directions.  This scale is called *jazz melodic minor*, as depicted in Example 11.3.

Ex. 11.3   **Jazz melodic minor scale**

## Turnarounds to Minor Tonics

Minor keys are constructed differently than their major counterparts, and therefore the ii and V chords are effected.

**Half-diminished Chords (ii⁰⁷)** • When a chord is built on the second scale degree of any minor key, it is half-diminished (Ø7) in quality.  A *half-diminished seventh chord* consists of a diminished triad with a minor seventh above the root (a diminished triad is analogous to a minor triad with a flatted 5th).  Half-diminished chords are also called *minor seven flat five chords* (MI⁷ᵇ⁵).  Example 11.4 shows the C minor scale and the resultant half-diminished ii chord.

Ex. 11.4   **C minor scale and half diminished ii chord**

The following facts pertain to extensions on half-diminished chords:
   1.  The diatonic ninth above a ii⁰⁷ chord is a minor ninth.  Many players consider this note too dissonant, and they substitute the root as an alternative, omitting

any ninth.

2. It is also possible to include a major ninth with a half-diminished chord. This note tends to pull towards a major tonic (it is the 3rd of a major I) and must resolve down before cadencing.

3. Players often add a diatonic fourth (or 11th) to half-diminished chords. As is the case with MI⁷ chords, the perfect 4th is consonant in this context. In this instance, the 3rd of the chord is actually omitted in arpeggiation or chord-voicing.

Example 11.5 depicts the usage of 9ths and 4ths over half-diminished chords.

**Ex. 11.5   Adding 9ths and 4ths to half diminished chords**

**Scale** • When a half-diminished chord functions as ii⁷ to a minor tonic, it is appropriate to use the natural minor scale of that key (i.e. D⁰⁷ uses a C natural minor scale from D-D). Example 11.6 displays the natural minor scale one step down for a half-diminished seventh chord (also referred to as the Locrian mode).

**Ex. 11.6   ii⁰⁷ uses natural minor scale of tonic**

The above scale can be altered to include the major ninth above the root, as in Example 11.7. The resultant scale is actually the same as F jazz melodic minor, arising from the fact that Dᵒ⁷ and FMI⁶ contain exactly the same tones!

**Ex. 11.7   ♮9th of scale for half diminished**

**Altered Dominant Ninth Chords** • When a chord is built on the fifth degree in a minor key, a minor seventh chord results. However, in jazz and classical music this chord is almost always altered to be a dominant seventh. The V chord in minor must be a dominant seventh in order to create the sound of a cadence when progressing to i. Example 11.8 shows the non-tonal vMI⁷-i, followed by the correctly altered V⁷-i which is used in jazz turnarounds.

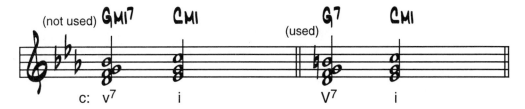

Ex. 11.8   Non tonal v (MI⁷) and tonal V (dominant 7) for minor keys

V⁹ in a minor key cannot feature a major ninth, as this note is out of the key signature. It is almost universal to raise or lower the ninth of a V chord to a minor tonic by a half step. The resultant chords can be described as *seven flat-nine* (7♭9) or *seven sharp-nine* (7♯9) chords. Curiously enough, dominant chords are the only chords in jazz which typically feature non-major ninths. Example 11.9 outlines the C⁷♭9 and C⁷♯9 chords.

Ex. 11.9   C⁷⁽♭9⁾ and C⁷⁽♯9⁾ chords

**Scales •** A dominant 7♭9 chord employs the harmonic minor scale for the key in which it functions as V (i.e. G⁷♭9 uses C harmonic minor, from G to G, because this chord is V in the key of C).

A dominant 7♯9, on the other hand, sounds best when played with the melodic minor scale a half step up from the root, a scale containing all of the chord tones (except for the often-omitted fifth). When using this scale, a flatted fifth is emphasized.

Example 11.10 displays the scales for G⁷♭9 and G⁷♯9 chords.

Ex. 11.10   Scales for dominant chords with altered ninths

**Resolution** • When a half-diminished ii chord progresses to $V^7$ with an altered ninth, the same principles of resolution apply as to other circle-of-fifth progressions (7-3, 9-5, 3 becomes 7).

**Smooth Arpeggiation** • As was the case with turnarounds to major tonics, it is likewise possible to resolve the seventh of a $ii^{\varnothing 7}$ and retain the other pitches as common tones. If the $ii^{\varnothing 7}$ is arpeggiated with a root (and no ninth), the resulting V chord will automatically be $V^{7\flat 9}$. Example 11.11 displays the smooth arpeggiation from $ii^{\varnothing 7}$ to $V^{7\flat 9}$.

Ex. 11.11  Smooth arpeggiation for ii - V in minor

**Formula: 3rd to Flat 9th Lines** • *3rd to flat 9th lines* are among the most commonly played figures over dominant harmony. In these lines, the 3rd of the dominant chord leads directly to the flatted 9th. Next, the line can resolve by step into the 5th of the tonic chord, or continue down the scale to the 7th of the dominant chord, which will, of course, resolve to the 3rd of the tonic. Example 11.12 illustrates 3rd to flat 9th lines.

Ex. 11.12  3rd to ♭9 lines resolving to tonic

Arpeggiation from 3rd to ♭9th is likewise effective, as shown in Example 11.13.

**Ex. 11.13  Arpeggiation from 3rd to ♭9**

The above formulae are based on the harmonic minor scale of the tonic, which can be used to highlight the 3rd and flat 9th.  Harmonic minor can also be used to produce a hybrid be-bop dominant scale.  These usages are displayed in Example 11.14.

**Ex. 11.14  Harmonic minor (be-bop) scale**

## The Turnback Progression

The *turnback progression* emphasizes the tonic chord of a major key through the circle of fifths.  This progression consists of the chords I-VI⁷⁽♭⁹⁾-ii⁷-V⁷, and its purpose is to "turn back" to tonic.  Tunes can begin with the turnback progression, and any tune which begins on the tonic chord will employ the turnback progression in the last two bars of each chorus.  3rd-to-flat-9th lines effectively outline the dominant chords of the turnback progression, as seen in Example 11.15.

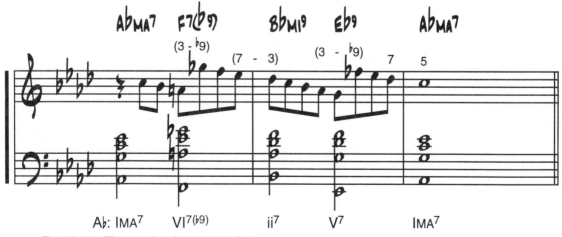

**Ex. 11.15  The turnback progression**

**Exercises**

1. Construct half-diminished 7th chords from root to 7th on D, G, A, F♯, and C♯.
2. Reconstruct the chords above with fourths replacing thirds.
3. Construct dominant 7♭9 chords from 3rd to ninth on G, A, C, F, and B♭.
4. Construct dominant 7♯9 chords from 3rd to 9th (omit 5th) on E, A♭, D♭, C♯ and G.
5. Notate chords for arpeggiating iiø7-V7♭9 in the following minor keys: C, A, F, E, and G. Use smooth arpeggiation so that only one note changes between ii and V.
6. Prepare and employ a practice sheet for the tune *Get Out The Rake*, using smooth arpeggiation for ii-V progressions. Practice solo choruses using 3rd-♭9 formula and other applicable elements of style.
7. Prepare and employ a practice sheet to *You Again*.. Make sure chords are notated for smooth ii-V arpeggiation. Memorize the practice sheet and work on improvised solos.
8. Practice 3rd to flat 9th lines and descending harmonic minor scales over dominant chords as assigned by the instructor.
9. Practice the turnback melody line from Example 11.15 (on next page) in all keys.
10. Analyze the sample solo to *Get Out The Rake* (Appendix 2), identifying

## Get Out The Rake

SEE APPENDIX 1 FOR B♭, E♭, AND
BASS CLEF TRANSPOSITIONS

## You Again

SEE APPENDIX 1 FOR B♭, E♭, AND BASS CLEF TRANSPOSITIONS

CHAPTER 12

# Turnarounds to ii and vi in Major Keys
## The Altered Dominant Chord

### Turnaround to Supertonic (ii)

It has been established that the circle-of-fifths is a commonly used device by composers of standard songs. The progression iii-vi-ii-V-I is particularly prevalent. In this progression, if the vi chord is altered to become a dominant seventh (as opposed to the diatonic minor 7th), then the iii and VI chords effect a turnaround to the ensuing ii. In other words, iii and VI sound like a ii-V progression, leading to the actual ii chord of a key. For instance, in the key of F major, the chords $A_{MI}^9$-$D^{13}$-$G_{MI}^9$ can be described as iii-VI-ii, but the $A_{MI}^9$ and $D^{13}$ chords have a ii-V relationship to $G_{MI}^9$ (see Example 12.1). The progression $iii^{\varnothing 7}$-$VI^{7(\flat 9)}$-$ii^7$-$V^7$-I is typically used to end songs and strongly resembles the turnback progression from the preceding chapter.

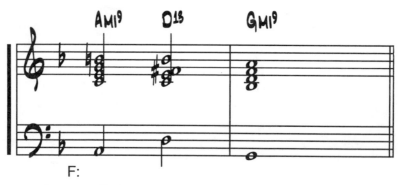

Ex. 12.1   iii - VI - ii

Because the ii chord of any major key is a minor chord, it is desirable to alter iii and VI in the typical manner for turnarounds to minor tonics. So in the key of F major, iii can be changed from $A_{MI}^7$ to $A^{\varnothing 7}$; and VI can be altered from $D^7$ to $D^{7\flat 9}$, as seen in Example 12.2.

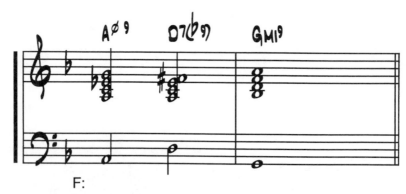

Ex. 12.2   Alternate iii - VI - ii

When the preceding progression is used, the ii chord is not actually tonicised because its minor 7th quality leads it onward towards V$^7$ in the key. However, using iii$^{Ø7}$ and VI$^{7\flat9}$ *does* create a strong circle-of-fifths pull towards the ii chord.

## Turnaround to Sub-mediant (vi)

The most commonly-tonicised chord (other than I) in a key is IV (see Chapter 10), but it is also common for composers to tonicise vi. [A tonicisation is achieved by placing a ii and a V in front of any major or minor chord.] The vi chord in any major key is a minor triad, so its ii chord will usually be half-diminished and its dominant will usually contain an altered ninth. Example 12.3 displays the turnaround to the vi chord in the key of E♭ major.

Ex. 12.3  Turnaround to vi

Notice that the ii chord (of vi) is built on the leading tone of the key in which the vi chord functions. In this case the key is E♭ and the turnaround to vi is initiated with a D$^{Ø7}$ chord.

When tonicising either ii or vi, the principles of turnarounds to minor tonics (discussed in Chapter 11) apply.

**Formula: Finding the Chromatics** • When a turnaround to ii or vi is played, in each case the third of the dominant chord is not diatonic to the actual key. For instance, in Example 12.1, the third of the D$^{13}$ (F♯) is not a tone in the key of F major. Likewise, in Example 12.3, the third of G$^7$ (B) is not a diatonic pitch to the key of E♭ major. These pitches are chromatic to the keys in which they are played. The turnaround to the IV chord (described in Chapter 10) features a dominant chord in which the seventh is chromatic to the key.

Finding the chromatics can be described as seeking out and emphasizing these 3rds and 7ths of chords that are not in the key of the song. It is essential for the improviser to treat these tones as primary goal notes for "making the changes." The chromatic 3rd or 7th is almost always the first note emphasized by a soloist at the appropriate points in a progression. Example 12.4 displays the principle of finding the chromatics in turnarounds to ii and vi.

**Ex. 12.4 "Finding the chromatics" : turnarounds to ii and vi**

## The Altered Dominant Chord (ALT)

The altered dominant chord contains three or four altered tones and is indicated by "ALT" (i.e. CALT, FALT). This chord can contain either a sharped 9th or flatted 9th, or both. The flatted 13th is present as well. It may also contain a flatted 5th (#11). Example 12.5 displays some typical voicings of altered dominant chords.

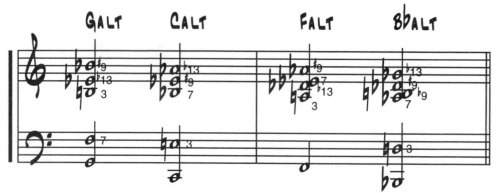

**Ex. 12.5 Altered dominant chord voicings**

[Note: These voicings are made clear by positioning the 7th and 3rd directly over the root, with most of the extensions placed above.]

Example 12.6 shows some hybrid scales constructed to accommodate altered dominant harmony.

**Ex. 12.6  Hybrid scales for altered dominant harmony**

Jazz improvisers will alter dominant chords at will in order to create interesting consonant tones. In other words, any dominant seventh chord, functioning as $V^7$, can become an altered dominant at the discretion of the performer.

**Smooth Arpeggiation** • Smooth arpeggiation from $ii^9$ to $V^{13}$ (Chapter 10) can be varied to employ tones in the altered dominant chord. If the 9th of the ii chord is lowered a half step, it becomes the ♭13th of the V. Likewise, it the 5th of the ii chord is lowered a half step, it becomes the ♭9th of the V. Example 12.7 demonstrates smooth arpeggiation from $ii^9$ to $V^{13}$ with altered tones.

**Ex. 12.7  Smooth arpeggiation to altered dominants**

**Formula: The Altered Dominant Cell** • The simplest way to effect the altered dominant sound in improvisation is through employing the *altered dominant cell*, which consists of the root, altered ninths, 3rd, and 7th of the dominant chord. These tones are quite easily located, since the ♭9th is a half step above the root and the ♯9th is a half step below the 3rd of the dominant chord. Example 12.8 demonstrated usage of the altered dominant cell with 7th to 3rd resolution into the tonic chord.

**Ex. 12.8  The altered dominant cell (resolving to tonic)**

**Formula: Altered Dominant Lick** • The *altered dominant lick* is a descending, triplet-arpeggio figure which makes use of the altered dominant tones. It contains both the sharped and flatted ninths, and the flatted 13th. Example 12.9 illustrates the altered dominant lick and its usage in melody.

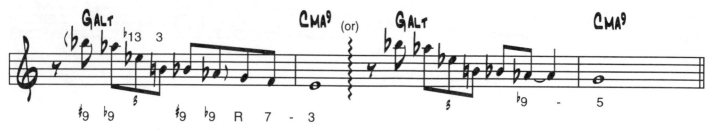

**Ex. 12.9  The altered dominant lick**

**Term: Solo Break** • A *solo break* is played by a soloist at the end of the original melody of a tune. This statement becomes a lead-in to the first chorus.

The factors pertinent to a solo break are as follows:
1. The break is almost always two bars in duration, as the band abruptly stops playing at the 30th bar of the tune and allows two bars of silence (a break) for the soloist.
2. The absence of accompaniment allows the soloist to create his own chord progression for the break:
   a. The most common progression is I-VI-ii-V (the turnback).
   b. A break can also be played entirely over the tonic chord.
   c. Other progressions are possible.
3. Solo breaks are generally linear, as opposed to using licks, even if the solo which follows is lick-oriented.
4. The soloist usually allows at least one beat of silence before embarking on the solo break.

Example 12.10 demonstrates some characteristic solo breaks.

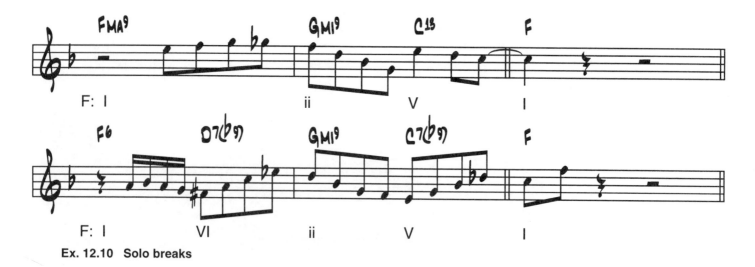

**Ex. 12.10  Solo breaks**

**Exercises**

1. Construct turnaround lines to the ii chord in the following major keys (each chord one measure in duration): A♭, E♭, G, D.
2. Construct turnaround lines to the vi chord for the keys listed in Exercise 1.
3. Construct lines for the progression iii$^{\varnothing 7}$-VI$^{7♭9}$-ii$^7$-V$^7$-I, with each chord lasting two beats, in the following keys: C, F, B♭.
4. Notate and practice the altered dominant cell in all keys.
5. Notate and practice the altered dominant lick in all keys.
6. Find the chromatic tones for the following chords in the key of D♭ major: F$^7$, B♭$^7$, E♭$^7$.
7. Prepare and employ a practice sheet for the tune *Grapes and Flowers* (on p. 70).
8. Compose a solo to *Grapes and Flowers* employing characteristic formula, hybrid scales, altered dominant tones and licks, and emphasizing the chromatics.
9. Improvise to *Grapes and Flowers* with emphasis on altered dominant figures and minor turnaround figures.
10. Analyze the sample solo to *Grapes and Flowers* (Appendix 2), identifying characteristic jazz formulae and altered dominant figures.

## Grapes and Flowers

SEE APPENDIX 1 FOR Bb, Eb, A...
BASS CLEF TRANSPOSITIO...

CHAPTER 13

# Diminished Seventh Chords and Scales
# X°

variant symbols:  XDIM, X°7

## Construction

The *diminished seventh chord* (or fully diminished seventh chord) is constructed of consecutive minor thirds over a chord root.  It is analogous to a minor seventh chord with the fifth and seventh flatted.  The difference between a diminished seventh chord and a *half* diminished seventh chord is the seventh, which is a half step higher in the latter.  Both chords contain a diminished triad (the same as a minor triad with a flatted fifth).  Example 13.1 displays a diminished seventh chord.

**Ex. 13.1  Diminished seventh chord**

The diminished seventh chord is *symmetrical* because any note in the chord can be the root.  Example 13.2 shows that the diminished seventh chords built on B, D, E♯, and G♯ are actually identical.

**Ex. 13.2  Symmetry of diminished seventh chords**

Due to its symmetrical nature, the diminished seventh chord is the *only* chord in the jazz vocabulary that never contains a ninth.  And also because of symmetry, there are only three different diminished seventh chords!

## Function

**Dominant** • A diminished seventh chord will function as dominant harmony to the chord a half step up. In this case, the diminished chord is said to be built on the *leading tone* to its tonic. Example 13.3 shows a diminished seventh chord functioning as dominant.

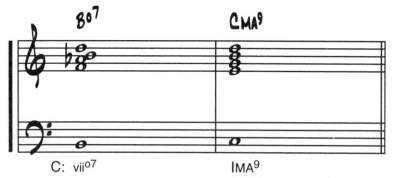

Ex. 13.3 °7 chord functioning as dominant (vii - I)

A leading tone chord (°7) will often be placed between two chords whose roots are a step apart, as depicted in Example 13.4 (in this case, it can be seen that ♯I°7 substitutes for VI$^{7(♭9)}$ in a turnback progression).

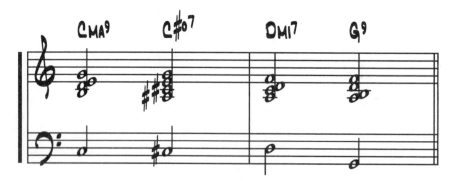

Ex. 13.4 °7 leading tone chord between two chords a step apart

**Embellishing** • In jazz music, diminished seventh chords often embellish the chords which follow them, with the two chords sharing a common tone. Example 13.5 depicts two usages of embellishing diminished chords.

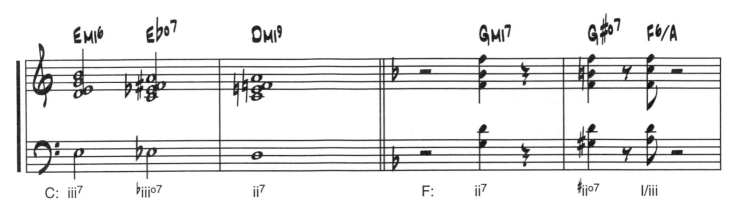

**Ex. 13.5 Embellishing °7 chords**

The first progression in Example 13.5 above finds ♭iii°7 substituting for VI7 in the circle of fifths. The second progression has been dubbed the *Count Basie ending*, for the noted bandleader and pianist, Bill "Count" Basie.

**IV-♯IV°7-I (The IV-I Idiom)** • In jazz progressions, IV is often used to precede tonic at non-cadential points. Frequently a ♯IV°7 chord will be inserted between IV and I for embellishment (as in Example 13.5, ♯IV°7 and I share a common tone). When this progression occurs, it is usual for the tonic chord to be played with the 5th in the bass. Example 13.6 displays this progression, which is one of the IV-I idioms (see Chapters 14 and 15 for the others). Examine the tune *Parts of You* to find a usage of the IV-♯IV°7-I idiom.

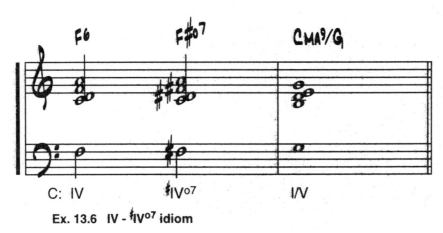

**Ex. 13.6 IV - ♯IV°7 idiom**

**Scale: Diminished (Octatonic)** • The *diminished scale* is preferred for diminished harmony and is constructed of alternating whole and half steps, or vice versa. The diminished scale contains eight notes, one more than a major or minor scale. When used for diminished seventh chords in jazz, the scale almost always begins with a whole step. Example 13.7 shows the construction of a diminished scale.

**Ex. 13.7  Diminished (octatonic) scale for diminished harmony**

Note that every other note in the diminished scale is a tone of the diminished seventh chord, while the remaining notes form a different diminished seventh chord.

## Consonance

All the tones of the diminished scale are consonant with diminished seventh harmony, as the scale contains only chord tones and the notes one step above each. The non-chord tones are the most expressive notes of the scale for improvising. Any note outside of the diminished scale will not be consonant.

## Using Diminished Chords with Dominant 7ths

The notes from 3rd to 9th of a dominant seventh chord with a flatted ninth ($7^{\flat 9}$) form a diminished seventh chord!  Example 13.8 displays this diminished seventh chord contained within the dominant. In this example, $F^7$ functions as V in B♭, and the A°7 chord contained within is vii⁷ (or leading tone) harmony in the same key.

**Ex. 13.8  °7 chord contained within dominant 7($^{\flat}$9)**

The improviser can therefore use the diminished scale when playing to dominant harmony. In this case, the scale will begin with a half step from the root of the dominant chord and continue alternating with whole steps (contrary to its use with diminished seventh chords, where the whole step comes first). Example 13.9 displays the F diminished scale for $F^7$ harmony.

**Ex. 13.9  Diminished scale for dominant  harmony (begins with 1/2 step)**

Because of symmetry, the scale above is also used for three other dominant chords in ascending minor 3rds from F (A♭, B, and D).

A study of the tones in the diminished scale reveals that it is entirely consonant for dominant harmony, containing the root, ♭9, ♯9, 3rd, ♭5th, 5th, 13th, and 7th of the chord.

**Formula: Lines Based on the Diminished Scale** • The diminished scale is one of the few scales that is effective in and of itself for jazz improvisation.  It can be employed in the following ways:
1.  The scale can be played as a scale, in consecutive order.
2.  The scale consists only of the tones of the diminished seventh chord and the notes one step above each (or half step below each).  The non-chord tones can be used as auxiliaries to embellish the chord tones.

Example 13.10 displays the auxiliary relationship of tones in the diminished scale to the tones of the diminished seventh chord.

**Ex. 13.10  Relationship of diminished scale to chord tones**

Example 13.11 displays a variety of sequential melody figures created by using the non-chord tones in the diminished scale as auxiliaries to the diminished seventh chord tones.

**Ex. 13.11  Sequential patterns using diminished scales (chord tones circled)**

The lines above can be employed effectively with dominant and diminished harmony, and because of symmetry, each line is usable for four different diminished seventh and four different dominant seventh chords!  For instance, the figures in Example 13.11 can be played over C°7, Eb°7, F♯°7, and A°7, as well as B7, D7, F7, and Ab7; because each of these chords contains a common diminished seventh chord.

Example 13.12 features a melodic phrase which is not a sequential pattern, but is based on the above-described principles for using the diminished scale.  This phrase could be played to dominant chords built on C, Eb, F♯, or A; and diminished chords built on C♯, E, G, or Bb.

**Ex. 13.12  Non-sequential line employing diminished scale tones**

### Exercises

1.  Construct the following diminished 7th chords and scales: C♯°7, F°7, D♯°7, B°7.
2.  Construct a sequential line for each of the chords in Exercise 1.
3.  Resolve the chords in Exercise 1, as both dominant function and embellishing diminished 7ths to other chords.
4.  Practice the three diminished chords and scales, beginning on the roots of each applicable dominant and diminished chord (there will be four dominant and four diminished chords, all using the same material).
5.  Practice and memorize the sequential lines from Example 13.11 for all three diminished scales.
6.  Prepare and employ a practice sheet for the tune *Parts of You*, using diminished scales where appropriate.
7.  Compose a solo to *Parts of You*, employing altered dominant idioms and diminished formulae.

8. Practice improvising to *Parts of You*,, using diminished scales and figures over diminished and dominant harmony.
9. Analyze the sample solo to *Parts of You* (Appendix 2), identifying characteristic jazz formulae and diminished idioms.

## Parts of You

SEE APPENDIX 1 FOR B♭, E♭, AND BASS CLEF TRANSPOSITIONS

CHAPTER 14

# "Rhythm" Changes
## ii-Chord Substitution

## "Rhythm" Changes

The chord progression to Gershwin's *I've Got Rhythm* is the second most often-played progression in jazz (behind the 12-bar blues). It is in the standard, 32-bar song form and represents a challenge to all improvisers. The song, ***Rhythm Changes***, (page 83), is written to the *I've Got Rhythm* progression.

**The "A" Section** • It is the "A" section of the *I've Got Rhythm* progression where the real challenge lies. The main difficulty is the fast harmonic rhythm (that is to say, the speed at which the chord change) of two beats per chord.

An analysis of the "A" section reveals the following:

1.  The first four measures consist of two circle-of-fifth turnback progressions for tonic emphasis. The VI dominant chord in the turnback progression strengthens the pull towards the ii chord.
2.  Measures 5 and 6 represent a turnaround to the IV chord, followed by a IV-I idiom (see Chapter 13).
3.  Measures 7 and 8 feature a re-emphasis of tonic, again through the circle-of-fifths.

Some helpful concepts towards improvising to the "A" section are as follows:

1.  For the first four bars, licks "in the key" can be effective, especially those based on the pentatonic/blues scale. It is not essential to outline every chord each time these bars are played.
2.  When all chords are outlined, the 3rd (B♮) of the VI$^7$ chord (G$^7$) is chromatic to the key and is the primary goal note. [Note: for any VI dominant, the 3rd of the chord is a half step above tonic in the key.]
3.  The VI dominant usually contains altered ninths because this is a turnback progression. Lines featuring the 3rd and flatted 9th of the chord are most appropriate (see Chapter 11).
4.  In measure 3, a iii$^7$ chord is interchangeable with I, having little effect on the improvisation because these chords share common tones.
5.  Measure 5 should emphasize the flatted 7th of the key (A♭) in order to affect the turnaround to the IV chord. This note resolves to the 3rd of the IV chord (G) in measure 6 (see Chapter 10).
6.  It seems most satisfying to conclude the "A" section with lick-oriented ideas, as opposed to linear playing. Again, the pentatonic/blues scale serves well. This

practice is especially important for the last measure of the second "A" section, where the harmonic rhythm is too quick for the chords to be outlined.

An analysis of the sample solo (Appendix 2) exemplifies these concepts.

Example 14.1 depicts some goal notes and the resolutions found in the "A" section of *Rhythm Changes*.

**Ex. 14.1   Goal notes for "Rhythm Changes" "A" section**

**Formula: Descending Melodic Gesture, measures 5-6** • Measures 5 and 6 of the *I've Got Rhythm* progression contain an ascending bass line featuring scale degrees 1, 3, 4, #4, and 5. A typical melodic gesture is based around the descending pitches 1, ♭7, 6 (3rd of the IV chord), ♭6, and 5. Example 14.2 depicts a line derived from this melodic formula.

**Ex. 14.2   Descending goal notes for mm. 5-6 of "A" section**

**Diminished 7th Chord Substitution** • It is typical for improvisers to play substitute °7 chords in measures 1 and 2, replacing VI⁷ with #I°⁷, and V⁷ with #ii°⁷. The resulting progression is I-#I°⁷-ii-#ii°⁷. This substitution can be effective whether or not the rhythm section follows suit. Example 14.3 demonstrates this substitute progression.

**Ex. 14.3  Substitute dd7 chords for mm. 1-2 of "A" section**

**IV-ivMI⁷ (or MI⁶)-I (IV-I idiom)** • As mentioned above, measures 6 and 7 of the "A" section contain the IV-I idiom (IV-♯IV°⁷-I, as described in Chapter 13). A second IV-I idiom uses the chord IV-ivMI⁷ (or MI⁶)-I, in which a minor iv chord substitutes for ♯iv°⁷ (i.e. E♭MI⁷ (or E♭MI⁶) in place of E°⁷). These two permutations of the IV-I idiom are always interchangeable in improvisation. Example 14.4 depicts a melody using this alternate IV-I idiom.

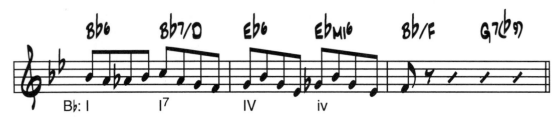

**Ex. 14.4  Substituting iv for ♯iv°⁷**

A look back at *Parts of You* (Chapter 13) reveals an opportunity for this same substitution in the second ending.

**The Bridge** • The bridge of *Rhythm Changes* is much simpler to negotiate in that the harmonic rhythm expands to one chord for every two measures. It can easily be analyzed as beginning on III dominant, and passing through the other dominant chords in the circle of fifths, concluding with V⁷.

The key elements of improvising to the bridge are as follows:

1. The first three chord-3rds are chromatic to the key, and are the primary goal notes (D⁷-F♯, G⁷-B, C⁷-E).
2. 7ths will resolve to 3rds, as in all circle-of-fifth progressions.
3. Because each chord is dominant in quality, 3rds do not remain stationary to become 7ths, but rather resolve down by a half step to them.

Example 14.5 outlines the goal notes and resolutions found in the bridge of *Rhythm Changes*.

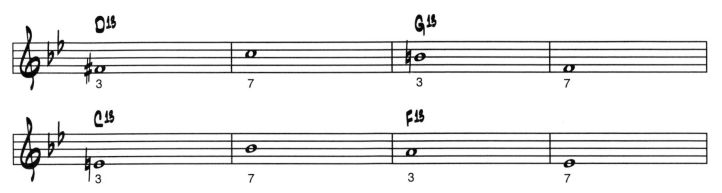

**Ex. 14.5   Goal notes for bridge**

**ii-Chord Substitution** • ii-chord substitution is the practice of superimposing a $ii^7$ chord when a progression contains a prolonged dominant 7th harmony.  For instance, $G^7$ functions as $V^7$ in the key of C.  When a progression features a lengthy $G^7$ chord, the applicable ii-chord substitute is $DMI^7$ (the $ii^7$ chord in C).  ii-chord substitution is possible whether or not the dominant chord resolves to its tonic.  By using ii-chord substitution, an improviser can create additional turnaround (ii-V) opportunities where the basic harmony has not allowed for such.  Example 14.6 demonstrates the ii-chord substitution.

**Ex. 14.6   ii chord substitution**

Example 14.7 features a melodic line without ii-chord substitution.  The melody utilizing a substitute harmony is more progressive or modern-sounding.

**Ex. 14.7   Melody without ii chord substitution**

Example 14.8 illustrates the possible ii-chord substitutes for the bridge of *Rhythm Changes*.

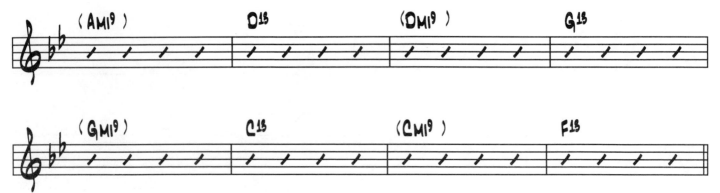

**Ex. 14.8  ii chord sustitutions for the bridge**

Although each dominant chord above can be played with ii-chord substitution, it is not a universal practice for improvisers to do so.  More commonly, the performer will play one or two of the dominant chords without using substitutions.  In this way, each chorus can feature choices by the soloist.  The sample solo in Appendix 2 demonstrates the concept of selective ii-chord substitution.

**Exercises**

1. Name the ii-chord substitutes for the following chords: $A\flat^7$, $B^7$, $D\flat^7$, $E^7$, $B\flat^7$.
2. Compose two licks "in the key" for the first four bars of *Rhythm Changes*.
3. Compose a solo to the "A" section of *Rhythm Changes* using the goal notes provided in Example 14.1 (page 79).  The rhythmic placement of the goal notes can be altered to suit your solo.
4. Compose a line, moving predominantly in eighth-notes, to the bridge of *Rhythm Changes*, in which 7ths resolve to 3rds as the chords change.
5. Prepare and employ a practice sheet to *Rhythm Changes*, choosing ii-chord substitutes for the bridge.
6. Transcribe and/or analyze a solo to the *I've Got Rhythm* progression from a recorded performance.
7. Practice improvising to the *I've Got Rhythm* progression using goal notes provided in this chapter.
8. Practice the bridge to the *I've Got Rhythm* progression using altered dominant and diminished figures.

## Rhythm Changes

SEE APPENDIX 1 FOR B♭, E♭, AND
BASS CLEF TRANSPOSITIONS

# SECTION 4

# Advanced Principles

CHAPTER 15

# Tritone Substitutions

## Second Ending Progressions

## Tritone Substitution

*Tritone substitution* refers to the fact that two dominant chords a tritone apart are interchangeable. [Note: a tritone is the interval of an augmented 4th or diminished 5th. It contains three whole steps, hence the name *tri*-tone.] Example 15.1 reveals the fact that two dominant chords a tritone apart, with flatted 5ths, are identical.

**Ex. 15.1   Identical chords a tritone apart**

Example 15.2 shows that the 3rd, 7th, and 9th of a dominant chord are identical to the 7th, 3rd, and ♭13th of the tritone substitute dominant, and furthermore that the all-important 3rds and 7ths are the same notes for both chords.

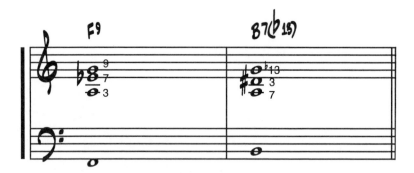

**Ex. 15.2   Identical chord tones**

Example 15.3 shows that the commonly-used keyboard voicing of a dominant 13th chord is a viable altered dominant voicing for the tritone substitute chord.

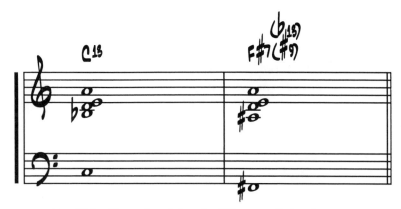

**Ex. 15.3  Shared voicing for tritone sub dominants**

**Function: Substitute Dominant** • A tritone-substituted dominant chord will function in the place of a $V^7$. In other words, the progression $ii^7$-$\flat II^7$-I can be substituted for $ii^7$-$V^7$-I, as seen in Example 15.4.

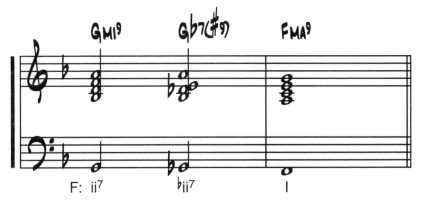

**Ex. 15.4  Tritone substitute turnaround**

Example 15.5 demonstrates a turnaround line with tritone substitution.

**Ex. 15.5  Turnaround melody with tritone substitution**

**Passing Chords •** The tritone substitute dominant is also used as a passing (or embellishing) chord, and can precede a major 7th, minor 7th, or other dominant 7th chord in most instances (notice that the passing chord is a half step above the following chord which it embellishes). It is not uncommon for improvisers to play both the $V^7$ and tritone substitute $\flat II^7$ before a tonic. Example 15.6 displays the usage of tritone substitute chords as embellishing a harmony.

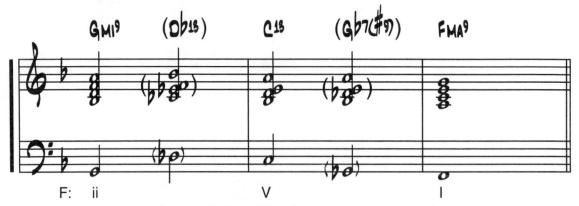

Ex. 15.6   Using tritone sub. for embellishment

In a similar manner, MI7 and ∅7 chords are often preceded with a MI7 embellishing chord up a half step, as demonstrated in Example 15.7.

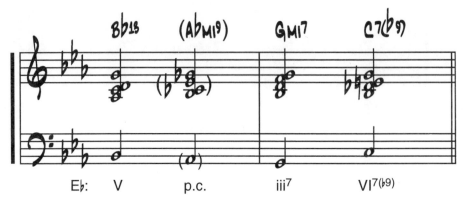

Ex. 15.7   Minor tritone substitute passing chord

Improvisation for tritone substitute passing chords is straightforward in that the new chord is superimposed onto existing harmony. In other words, simplistic lines which outline the passing chords will sound very progressive, even slightly "outside", to the prevailing harmony (see Example 15.8).

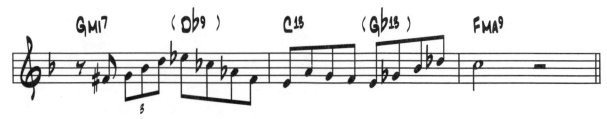

Ex. 15.8   Melody using tritone substitution

## Second Ending Progressions

Standard, 32-bar (AABA) song forms often contain first and second endings prior to the bridge. Charactertistically, the first ending will feature a turnback progression for the repeat of the "A" section. It is common for the second ending to contain two measures of a I[7] chord as a means of re-emphasizing tonic before the bridge. In these instances, a few substitute progressions are often employed for variety and continued harmonic motion.

**I-ii[7]-♯ii°[7]-I/III** • The most frequently-used second ending progression substitutes the chords I-ii[7]-♯ii°[7]-I/III in place of the indicated two measures of tonic harmony (♯ii[7] is an embellishing chord to I, as described in Chapter 13). This progression has a nice pull towards tonic, while affording the improviser some interesting chromaticism to play. Example 15.9 demonstrates this second-ending progression, which is typically employed for swing-tempo tunes.

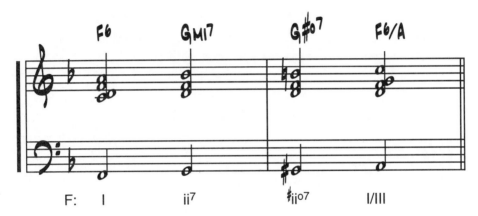

Ex. 15.9 Second ending progression

Example 15.10 shows the construction of a melody over the I-ii[7]-♯ii°[7]-I/III substitute progression.

Ex. 15.10   Melody for 2nd ending progression

In the example above, the goal notes move in parallel tenths against the bass line (bass: F, G, G♯, A; melody: A, B♭, B, C). The I-ii[7]-♯ii°[7]-I/III progression is actually usable in any instance where there is static major harmony for two measures or longer.

**I-ivMI⁷-I** • Another effective second-ending progression is analogous to the *plagal cadence* in classical music, and features the chords I-ivMI⁷-I, as depicted in Example 15.11 (ivMI⁶ can also be used). This progression is typically for ballad style songs.

Ex. 15.11   **Second ending progression using iv⁷**

The progression above can be embellished by adding a dominant seventh chord built on the flatted seventh scale degree (♭VII⁷). This chord is called *subtonic*, and the embellished progression is I-ivMI⁷-♭VII⁷-I (as seen in Example 15.12).

Ex. 15.12   **iv⁷ - ♭VII⁷ idiom**

It should be realized that the chords ivMI⁷ and ♭VII⁷ form a ii-V progression to the key up a minor 3rd from tonic. When playing these chords in the progression I-ivMI⁷-♭VII⁷-I, the seventh of the ♭VII⁷ can be resolved downward just as in a V-I progression. In this case, the seventh of the subtonic chord resolves to the fifth of the tonic chord, as was depicted in Example 15.12. The progression from ♭VII to I is otherwise known as a *deceptive resolution* (or deceptive cadence) of the dominant chord.

In that the plagal progression is employed in ballad style songs, improvisation usually involves sixteenth notes which connote a feeling of double-time swing (i.e. each measure of slow tempo "feels" like two measures of swing, at twice the tempo). In these instances (as seen in Example 15.13), the sixteenth notes are interpreted in a swinging style analogous to swing eighth notes.

**Ex. 15.13   Melody for 2nd ending progression in ballad style**

The improviser is free to add these second ending progressions whenever possible. These idioms are also used at other points in progressions when two consecutive measures of a major seventh chord are found.

### Exercises

1. Name the tritone substitutes for the following chords: D⁷, B⁷, G♭⁷, E⁷, F♯⁷.
2. Compose melodies to the second ending progression I-iiMI⁷-♯ii°⁷-I/III in the following keys: C, A♭, F, G.
3. Compose melodies, moving predominantly in sixteenth notes, to the second ending progression I-ivMI⁷-I for the keys in Exercise 3. The subtonic chord can be included.
4. Review the tunes *Mellotones* (page 45) and *Lacey Lady* (page 55), finding instances where tritone substitution and the second ending progressions can be added.
5. Practice turnaround progressions, employing tritone substitution for the dominant chords.
6. Review *Parts of You* (page 77), and practice improvisation using both functional and passing tritone substitution (for example, passing chords can be employed in the second halves of bars 2, 4, 6, 8, 10 and 12, while a functional ♭II⁷ chord can replace V⁷ in measure 16). Hint: try using B♭MI⁷ as the tritone substitute passing chord in measure 10.

CHAPTER 16

# Progressions from I to VI
## Tag Endings

## Progressions from I to VI

As discussed in Chapter 12, the VI chord (sub-mediant) is often a dominant harmony in the jazz context. It is typical for jazz tunes to progress from tonic to VI$^7$, setting up a ii-V-I cadence. In these instances various chords can be used to connect I to VI. These *I to VI progressions* are not to be confused with turnback progressions, where the tonic and VI$^7$ chords are each two beats in length. In the I to VI progressions, two to four measures are allotted.

**I-iii$^7$-VI$^7$** • The most basic connection to sub-mediant employs the iii$^7$ chord. This is a circle-of-fifths progression, and the iii$^7$ can be either a minor seventh or half-diminished seventh chord, as depicted in Example 16.1

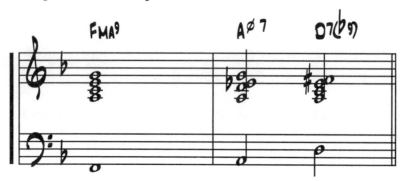

Ex. 16.1  I - iii$^7$ - VI$^7$

**I-ii$^7$-iii$^7$-VI$^7$** • The progression above can be embellished by adding a chord between tonic and iii$^7$. Supertonic (ii$^7$) is an acceptable passing chord, as seen in Example 16.2. These chords can be further embellished by inserting #ii$^{\circ 7}$ between ii and iii.

C: I    ii$^7$    #ii$^{\circ}$    iii$^7$    VI$^7$

Ex. 16.2  I - ii$^7$ - iii$^7$ - VI$^7$

**I-IV⁷-iii⁷-VI⁷** • Another connection can be made between tonic and iii⁷ with a chord built on the subdominant. The IV⁷, ivMI⁶, and iv⁷ chords are tritone substitute passing chords to iii⁷, as described in Chapter 15. Example 16.3 displays the progression I-IV⁷ (or ivMI⁷)-iii⁷-VI⁷.

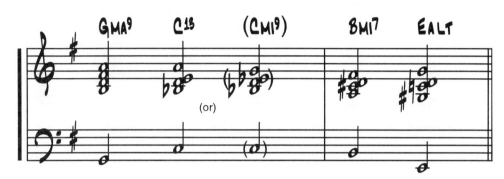

**Ex. 16.3  I - IV⁷ - iii⁷ - VI⁷**

**I-VII⁷-♭VII⁷-VI⁷** • Another method of connecting tonic to VI⁷ involves a descending chromatic progression of dominant chords: I-VII⁷-♭VII⁷-VI⁷. In this instance the ♭VII dominant is serving as a tritone substitute for iii⁷, as seen in Example 16.4.

**Ex. 16.4  I - VII⁷ - ♭VII7 - VI⁷**

**I-IV⁷-♭VII⁷-VI⁷** • A combination of above-described principles results in the chord progression I-IV⁷-♭VII⁷-VI⁷, as shown in Example 16.5. This connection is less common but equally effective as the others mentioned in this chapter.

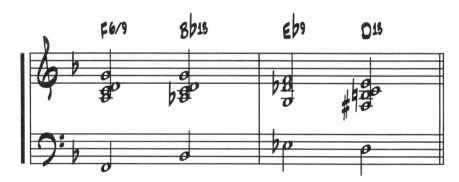

**Ex. 16.5  I - IV⁷ - ♭VII⁷ - VI⁷**

**Tritone Substitute for VI (♭III⁷)** • For any of the progressions above a tritone substitute chord (♭III⁷) can be used in place of the sub-mediant, as seen in Example 16.6.

Ex. 16.6   I - IV⁷ - iii⁷ - ♭III⁷

**I-♭iii⁷-♭VI⁷** • One other possible progression worthy of inclusion uses the chords down a half step from iii⁷ and VI⁷ as a substitute for them. The usage of these chords creates a turnaround progression a half step above ii and V in the key. Example 16.7 displays this chromatic alternative.

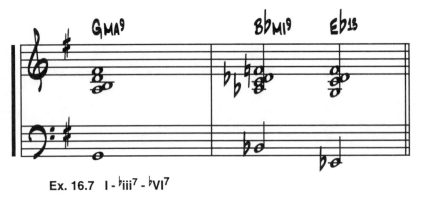

Ex. 16.7   I - ♭iii⁷ - ♭VI⁷

[Note: when a lead sheet indicates a I-VI progression, the improviser (and/or rhythm section) is free to employ any of the substitute progressions outlined above. It is equally effective for the improviser to play bluesy riffs in the key while the rhythm section executes one of the substitute progressions.]

## Tag Endings

A *tag* is an extension on the final cadence (turnaround progression) of a song. Tags are generally employed after the solos, when the head is being restated for the final time.

**Using iii and VI** • The typical tag ending is achieved by playing the iii and VI chords in place of the final tonic.  These chords, of course, lead back to ii and V in the circle-of-fifths, thereby delaying the end of the song.  Example 16.8 shows the usage of iii and VI to create a tag.

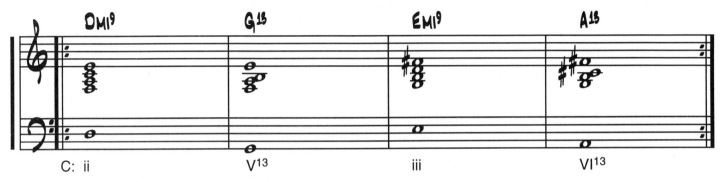

**Ex. 16.8  Tag ending**

The performers can improvise over the tag progression and repeat it a number of times at their discretion.  The song is usually concluded by sounding a staccato tonic chord, followed by a solo break of seven beats, and a final tonic on beat four of the last bar. Example 16.9 illustrates a characteristic solo break to conclude a tag ending.

**Ex. 16.9  Solo break for tag ending**

As shown above, the commonly used tonic at the conclusion of a tag ending is dominant 13th chord with a flatted 5th (or #11th).

**Using #iv°7 and iv7** • A tag which occurs less frequently employs #iv°7 and ivMI7 in place of ii and V.  When either tag is used, it is necessary to play ii and V for the final cadence.  Example 16.10 depicts the alternative tag progression. [Note: The tag progression indicated in this example can be used as yet another permutation of the I to VI progression, where #iv°7 is a tritone substitute for the tonic chord.]

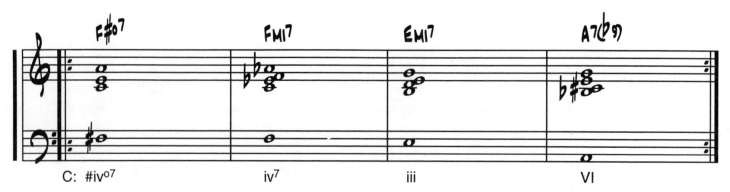

**Ex. 16.10  Alternate tag ending**

Some final thoughts on tag endings:

1. As is the case with I-VI progressions, the improviser can play bluesy figures throughout the tag progression.
2. The principles of tritone substitution and embellishing harmony can be applied to tag endings for diversity.
3. The soloist should indicate the end of the tag in preparation for the final statement of ii-V-I. This is normally accomplished through improvising a riff over the ii-V progression that can be sequenced up one step for the iii-VI, as an indication to the other players that the final ii-V-I is next. Example 16.11 displays a sequential line which could signal the end of a tag.

**Ex. 16.11  Sequential melody to signal end of tag**

## Exercises

1. Compose progressions connecting I to VI, as outlined in this chapter, in the following keys: C, F, E♭, G, and B♭. Notate the voicings on a treble staff over the bass notes in bass clef.
2. Compose melodies to the progressions of Exercise 1. In each case the chords can be either two beats or one measure in duration.
3. Practice and perform the tune *Paradoxy*, interchanging the progressions from tonic to submediant.
4. Prepare the tune *Tingle* as above. Practice a tag ending in class.
5. Using Roman numerals, analyze the progressions connecting I to VI in *Paradoxy* and *Tingle*.
6. Add a second-ending progression to *Tingle*.
7. Analyze the sample solos to *Paradoxy* and *Tingle* (Appendix 2), identifying characteristic jazz formulae and paying close attention to the treatment of I-VI progressions.

# *Paradoxy*

*SEE APPENDIX 1 FOR B♭, E♭, AND*
*BASS CLEF TRANSPOSITIONS*

# Tingle

SEE APPENDIX 1 FOR B♭, E♭, AND
BASS CLEF TRANSPOSITIONS

CHAPTER 17

# Harmony in Major Keys

## Major Keys

This book has shown that progressions in the standard jazz literature tend to fall into idioms that are replicated from tune to tune, and that the process of learning to improvise revolves around mastering these idioms. Listed below is a summary of the idioms for *major keys* discussed so far, in a hierarchy of frequency.

1. turnaround to tonic (I) - the cadence employed at the end of nearly every standard song, and at the end of "A" sections of most AABA tunes (Chapter 9).
2. turnaround to IV - used in about 75% of standard songs, this turnaround emphasizes the only diatonic chord that, when tonicised, seems to have achieved a real departure from the tonic of the song (Chapter 10).
3. turnarounds to ii and vi - well over 60% of jazz standards employ a turnaround to one or both of these chords (Chapter 12).
4. I-VI progressions and turnback progressions - the turnback is used by improvisers before each new chorus of a song beginning on the tonic chord; the I-VI progression is found in blues and standard songs (Chapters 14 and 16).
5. IV-I progression - this idiom is found in blues, *I've Got Rhythm*, other standard songs, and second endings of some AABA ballads (Chapters 13-15).
6. second ending progressions (Chapter 15)

There are other regularly occurring idioms in standard jazz literature. These are listed below in order of reiteration, and will be discussed in this chapter.

7. turnarounds to other diatonic chords -- iii and V.
8. turnarounds to chromatically altered chords.
9. modal borrowing - from the parallel minor.
10. step-down progression - tonicises the chord one step below.
11. circle of fifths.
12. modulation.
13. "the curve" - any chord or turnaround which cannot be analyzed as one of the above idioms.

**Turnarounds to iii and V** • The tonicisation of iii (submediant) is less regular than that of other diatonic chords because it requires chromatic harmony. The submediant is a minor 7th chord, so the progression which turns around to it is analogous to minor tonics. The turnaround to submediant is $\sharp IV^{\circ 7}$-$VII^7$-$iii^7$; see Example 17.1. Both the ii and V chords of this turnaround contain chromatic tones, these being the root of the $\sharp iv^{\circ 7}$ and the 3rd of the $VII^7$.

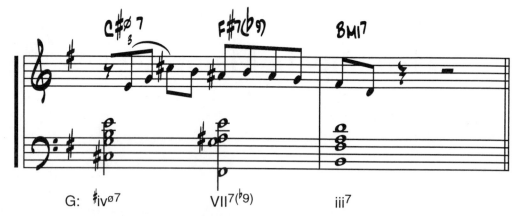

Ex. 17.1  Turnaround to iii$^7$ (in G major)

The turnaround to V also requires a chromatic alteration, and involves the chords vi$^7$-II$^7$-V. In this case, ii$^7$ is transformed into a dominant chord by raising the 3rd; see Example 17.2.

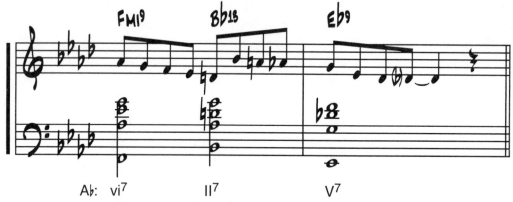

Ex. 17.2  Turnaround to V$^7$ (in A$\flat$ major)

The V chord rarely seems tonicised due to its tendency to pull towards the I (tonic) chord. As a result, the turnaround to V often leads to ii$^7$-V. This progression, vi$^7$-II$^7$-ii$^7$-V$^7$, doesn't actually tonicise the dominant, but rather anticipates a cadence on tonic (see Example 17.3).

Ex. 17.3  Turnaround to V, leading to ii - V

**Turnarounds to Chromatically Altered Chords and Modal Borrowing** • In major keys, any chord of minor 7th quality (i.e. ii⁷, iii⁷, vi⁷) can be altered to become a major 7th chord as the goal of a turnaround. These turnarounds to chromatically altered chords are effective because the progression can smoothly gravitate towards tonic through the circle of fifths. Example 17.4 shows a turnaround to the chromatically altered IIIMAJ⁷, and the smooth transition back towards tonic. [Note: Examples 17.1-17.4 demonstrate the principle of "finding the chromatics" to obviate the changes.]

**Ex. 17.4  Turnaround to chromatically altered IIIMA⁷**

*Modal borrowing* refers to using chords and turnarounds which appear in the parallel minor (for example, C major and C minor are parallel keys). The chords which are most frequently used (or tonicised by ii-V's) are the borrowed III and VI from the parallel minor. These appear as ♭III and ♭VI in the major key (see the discussion of minor keys in Chapter 18). Example 17.5 shows the diatonic chords from the minor mode, and how they appear in the parallel major.

**Ex. 17.5  Chords for modal borrowing**

**The Step-Down Progression** • The *step-down progression* begins with a major chord and results in a tonicisation down one step. This is accomplished by altering the major 7th chord to become a minor 7th chord, which will function as ii⁷ in a turnaround to a major chord one step down. *How High The Moon, I'll Remember April,* and *Ornithology* are examples of songs which begin with the step-down progression, as depicted in Example 17.6. In improvising to a step-down progression, it is typical to emphasize the 3rd (and/or 7th) of the major chord, which will be lowered a half step to make the transition to the minor 7th harmony.

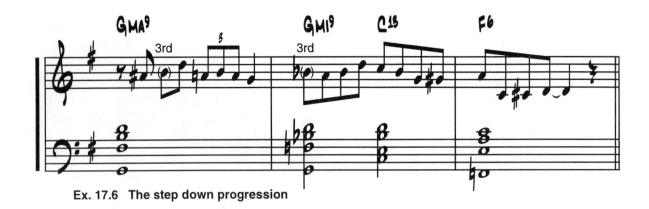

**Ex. 17.6 The step down progression**

**Diatonic Circle of Fifths •** There are two progressions referred to in jazz as the *diatonic circle of fifths,* but in actuality each of these contains one chromatic chord, and an alternation of diatonic and dominant harmonies. In some instances, a jazz tune will feature an entire diatonic circle-of-fifths progression.

One circle-of-fifths progression begins on ♯vi° (as in a turnaround to iii⁷) and progresses through the circle of fifths to the tonic chord. This entire progression is ♯iv°⁷-VII⁷-iii⁷-VI⁷-ii⁷-V⁷-I (see Example 17.7).

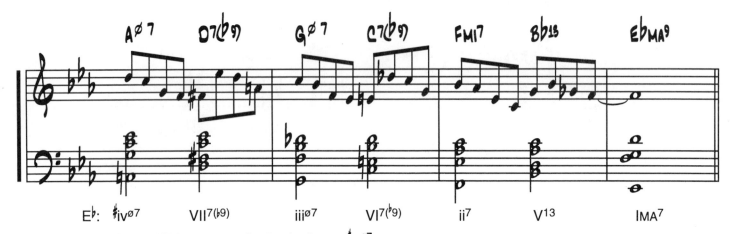

**Ex. 17.7 Circle of fifths progression beginning on ♯iv°⁷**

The other circle-of-fifths progression begins on the diatonic ivMI⁷ and employs a ♭VII⁷ in the progression towards tonic. This progression is iv⁷-♭VII⁷-iii⁷-VI⁷-ii⁷-V⁷-I, and is shown in Example 17.8.

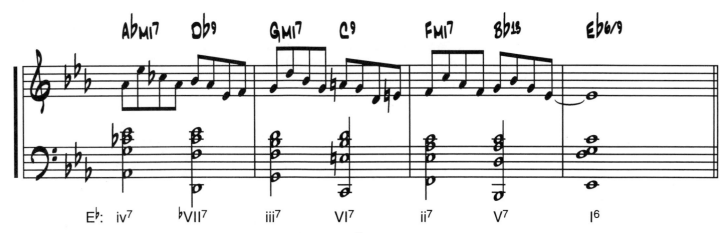

**Ex. 17.8  Circle of fifths progression beginning on iv⁷**

There are a few observations to be made about circle-of-fifths progressions:

1. The circle of fifths is a sequence of ii-V progressions, moving downward by step.
2. Improvisation to circle-of-fifth progressions may employ sequence, in which a ii-V melodic line is repeated, down a diatonic step for each set of two chords (as was demonstrated in Examples 17.7 and 17.8).
3. The chords with chromatically altered roots (i.e. ♯iv°⁷ or ♭VII⁷) are necessary to the circle-of-fifth progressions in that they create ii-V relationships with the chords around them.

**Modulation** • Modulation in jazz tunes occurs much less frequently than tonicisation. A modulation can be analyzed when several bars of a progression are clearly in a new key. This is contrasted with tonicisation, where a chord is tonicised by the ii and V chords preceding it. Generally speaking, when a jazz tune has modulated, the progression in the new key will be simple and circle-of-fifths related. Example 17.9 shows a progression which has modulated to the chromatically altered IIIᴍᴀ⁷, and then returns to tonic.

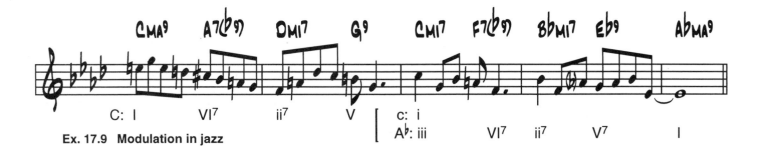

**Ex. 17.9  Modulation in jazz**

This chapter has outlined the harmonic idioms which are most likely to occur in the standard jazz lexicon. It should be noted that any composer is limited only by his or her imagination, and therefore other harmonic events are possible. It is usual to encounter "the curve" (a chord or relationship between two chords not explained above). However, improvisation, memorization, and transposition are all made easier when tunes are considered to be a combination of several, often-seen idioms, as opposed to 32 measures of unrelated chords.

### Exercises

1. Analyze the harmony of the tunes *Mellotones* (page 45), *Lacey Lady* (page 55), and *You Again* (page 63) in terms of the harmonic idioms found in each, rather than the individual chords (i.e. "turnaround to ii," "I-VI progression," "IV-I progression," etc.).
2. Analyze in terms of harmonic idioms the harmony of standard songs selected by the instructor.
3. Notate the chord symbols for turnarounds to $iii^7$ and V ($vi^7$-$II^7$-ii-$V^7$) in the following keys: F major, E♭ major, D♭ major, G major. Construct melody lines and improvise for each instance.
4. Compose and improvise turnaround melodies to $IIIMA^7$ and $VIMA^7$ in the following keys: A♭ major, D major, C major, B♭ major.
5. Notate the chord symbols to step-down progressions beginning on the following chords: $GMA^7$, $AMA^7$, and $FMA^7$. Compose lines and improvise to each.
6. Notate the chord symbols for both circle-of-fifth progressions in the following keys: C major, E♭ major, and B♭ major. Compose sequential melody lines for each instance.
7. Practice improvisation to the tune *Steps and Circles*, using techniques described in this chapter for step-down progressions, the circle of fifths, and turnarounds to chromatically altered harmonies.

# *Steps and Circles*

SEE APPENDIX 1 FOR B♭, E♭, AND
BASS CLEF TRANSPOSITIONS

CHAPTER 18

# Harmony in Minor Keys

Prior to the 1950's, the vast majority of standard songs were composed in major keys. Composers in the "funky" style of the 1950's and 60's (Benny Golson, Clifford Brown, Horace Silver, etc.) expanded the use of minor keys in jazz.

A review of minor keys reveals that major 7th chords are built on III and VI, while the minor chords are i and iv. The chord built on the fifth scale degree can be minor if tonicised by a turnaround, but will have dominant quality in the turnaround to tonic (I). The subtonic chord (VII[7]) is actually dominant in quality, and is V[7] of the relative major (III). As discussed in Chapter 11, the supertonic chord is half-diminished. Example 18.1 displays the chords of the minor mode, grouped by quality.

**Ex. 18.1  Chords in the minor mode**

As was the case for major keys (Chapter 17), there are harmonic idioms typical to tunes in the minor mode. They are listed as follows and will be discussed in this chapter:
1. turnaround to tonic (iMI[6]).
2. turnaround to iv - this is much like major keys, where I[7] is altered to become the dominant of iv. However, in minor keys iv[7] is a minor chord, so the turnaround to it is v[ø7]-I[7]-iv[7].
3. turnarounds to other diatonic chords - primarily III and VI, less frequently v and VII.
4. interchange with relative major - the III chord in minor *is* the tonic of relative major, and the diatonic VII[7] is dominant of III, so a turnaround to III seems like a modulation to the relative key. *Autumn Leaves* and *In Your Own Sweet Way* are examples of standard songs that alternate between relative keys.
5. minor turnback - the turnback in a minor key shares the same roots as the turnback for the parallel major. In this case the submediant chord is half-diminished and constructed over a chromatically raised root. The progression is iMI[6]-#vi[ø7]-ii[ø7]-V[7(♭9)].
6. VI[7]-V turnaround - in minor keys, a dominant-quality VI[7] chord often replaces ii in a turnaround.
7. ground bass pattern - a ground bass line descends from tonic to dominant, and is typically harmonized as i-i/VII-VI[7]-V[7]. The second chord in the pattern can be

either a tonic with the 7th in the bass, or a VII⁷ (dominant) chord.

8. the "whisper not" progression - moves from one minor chord to another, a perfect 4th down, using a modified ground bass (for example iv-iv/III-ii∅⁷-V⁷-i).
9. plagal cadence - a iv-i cadence at the end of some funky-style songs.

**Turnarounds to Diatonic Chords** • As with major keys, when songs contain minor tonicised diatonic chords, the principle of "finding the chromatics" is elemental to making the chord changes.

As discussed in Chapter 10, the turnaround to subdominant (iv) in the major mode requires emphasis on the flatted 7th in the key because it is the chromatic pitch. The minor mode requires that the 3rd of the tonic chord be raised in order for that chord to become a dominant. The raised 3rd of the key, therefore, is the essential chromatic note when improvising the turnaround to iv in minor (a secondary chromatic pitch is the 5th of the v∅⁷, which is a half step above tonic). Example 18.2 depicts a turnaround line to iv in the minor mode, with emphasis on the essential chromatic pitches.

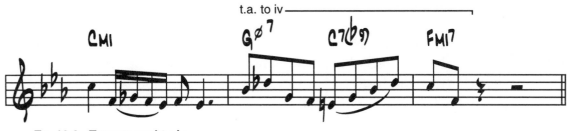

**Ex. 18.2  Turnaround to iv**

The turnaround to submediant (VI) begins on a subtonic chord (viiMI⁷-III⁷-VIMA⁷). Since the diatonic subtonic chord is major in quality, the chromatically lowered 3rd of that chord, which transforms it into a minor 7th, is the essential chromatic pitch for emphasis during improvisation; this pitch is also the 7th of the dominant chord that will follow. This note is a half step above tonic in the key. So, for example, a turnaround to VI in the key of F minor would emphasize the pitch G♭, which is the 3rd of the minor subtonic chord, E♭MI⁷. Example 18.3 depicts a turnaround melody to VI in F minor.

**Ex. 18.3  Turnaround to VI**

**Interchange with Relative Major** • The turnaround to relative major is entirely diatonic, so jazz tunes can pass smoothly back and forth between these two keys. A turnaround to relative major (III) requires simply the diatonic chords iv⁷-VII⁷-IIIMA⁷, as shown in Example 18.4.

**Ex. 18.4  Turnaround to relative major (III)**

**Turnback Progression in Minor** • It is not uncommon for tunes in the minor mode to begin and end with a turnback progression. As mentioned earlier, a raised submediant chord with half-diminished quality (♯viø⁷) is employed for the minor turnback. Obviously, the root of the ♯viø⁷ is a chromatic pitch, but that same note is the sixth above tonic minor (iMI⁶), so it doesn't actually sound chromatic (in fact, iMI⁶ and ♯viø⁷ are actually the same chord in different inversions). So it is typical for improvisers to play bluesy licks in the key over the entire turnback. Example 18.5 demonstrates this approach to improvising the turnback progression in minor (notice that iMI⁶ and ♯viø⁷ share all the same pitches). It should be noted that a tritone substitute for viø⁷ is possible in the turnback progression, resulting in a chord sequence of iMI⁶-III⁷ (dominant)-iiø⁷-V⁷⁽♭⁹⁾.

**Ex. 18.5  Turnback in minor**

**VI⁷ to V Turnaround** • A dominant chord built on submediant (VI⁷) is often employed to replace iiø⁷ in the minor turnaround to tonic. This chord can be considered a tritone substitute for ii. As is the case with the turnback progression, improvisation is typically "bluesy" in nature. Example 18.6 shows the VI-V-i turnaround and characteristic improvisation.

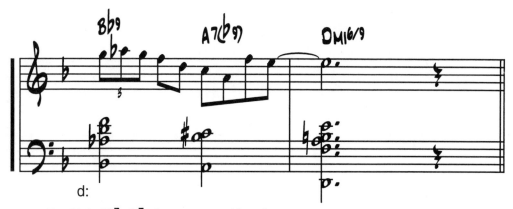

**Ex. 18.6   VI⁷ - V⁷ - i   turnaround in minor**

**The Ground Bass Pattern** • The *ground bass* pattern was popularized in the Baroque period of classical music, and features a stepwise descending bass line from tonic to dominant.  Again, improvisation is usually "bluesy" in nature since there is little chromaticism to exploit.  This progression is actually another type of turnback progression for minor keys, with VI⁷ substituting for iiø⁷.  Example 18.7 demonstrates the two permutations of the ground bass pattern.

**Ex. 18.7   Ground bass pattern**

**The "Whisper Not" Progression** • The *"Whisper Not" progression* comes from the Benny Golson composition of the same name and is a derivative of the ground bass pattern, employing a stepwise descending bass figure.  This chord series begins on a minor chord and ends by tonicizing another minor chord a perfect 4th below (typically iv-i or i-v).  Example 18.8 displays the "Whisper Not" progression as it appears in the original song.  In this usage, two "Whisper Not" patterns are joined together so that the final chord is the interval of a minor 7th below the starting point.

**Ex. 18.8 "Whisper Not" progression**

**Plagal Cadence** • The *plagal (church) cadence* is possible in major and minor keys, and consists of the subdominant chord followed by tonic harmony. This cadence, typically used in funky-style compositions, exploits the *auxiliary chord* relationship between iv and I. Any chord can be an auxiliary harmony to another chord a perfect 4th below because they share a common tone (the root of the second chord) and the other notes resolve by step, like auxiliary tones. Example 18.9 shows the plagal cadence in minor, and the auxiliary-chord relationship between iv and I.

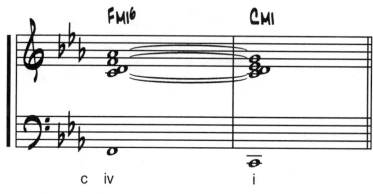

**Ex. 18.9 Plagal cadence**

The harmonic idioms above comprise the bulk of the chord choices for standard songs in minor keys. As is the case for major-key songs, any "curve" is possible when a composer exercises discretion to include atypical chords and idioms. It can be observed that songs in minor keys tend to be less chromatic and more "bluesy" than their major-key counterparts.

**12-Bar Blues in Minor (Minor Blues)** • The 12-bar blues progression in minor is analogous to that of major, with three 4-bar phrases. Like major blues, this progression begins on tonic, emphasizes subdominant in the fifth bar, and turns around back to tonic in the last phrase. A comparative analysis of minor blues is as follows:

1. The principle chords, $i^7$ and $iv^7$, are minor in quality (i can be $\text{MI}^6$ or $\text{MI}^{+7}$).
2. The iv chord is not used as often in measure 2, but a minor turnback may occupy the first two bars of the progression.
3. As in major, it is typical for minor blues to turnaround to the subdominant chord going from measure 4 to measure 5.
4. The "Whisper Not" progression frequently appears in mm. 5-6 as a means of progressing down a fourth from iv to i.
5. The final turnaround may be $ii^{ø7}$-$V^7$-i, but is more typically $VI^7$-$V^7$-i. It is not uncommon for measure 8 to contain a turnaround to the $VI^7$ chord in measure 9.
6. The i and iv chords can also have $\text{MI}^{11}$ quality, in which case the quartal and polyharmonic principles discussed in chapters 21 and 22 apply.

Diagram 18.1 is a blueprint for the 12-bar minor blues, with optional harmonies in parenthesis.

| $\mid i^7$ (#$vi^{ø7}$ | $\mid ii^{ø7}$ $V^7$) | $\mid i^7$ | $\mid (v^{ø7}$ $I^{7(\flat9)})$ $\mid$ |
| 1 | 2 | 3 | 4 |
| $\mid iv^7$ (/III | $\mid ii^{ø7}$ $V^7$) | $\mid i^7$ | $\mid (vii\text{MI}^7$ $III^7)$ $\mid$ |
| 5 | 6 | 7 | 8 |
| $\mid VI^7$ | $\mid (ii^{ø7})$ $V_{\text{ALT}}$ | $\mid i^7$ (#$vi^{ø7}$ | $\mid ii^{ø7}$ $V^{7(\flat9)})$ $\mid$ |
| 9 | 10 | 11 | 12 |

| $\mid F\text{MI}^7$ ($D^{ø7}$ | $\mid G^{ø7}$ $C^7$) | $\mid F\text{MI}^7$ | $\mid (C^{ø7}$ $F^{7(\flat9)})$ $\mid$ |
| 1 | 2 | 3 | 4 |
| $\mid B\flat\text{MI}^7$ (/A$\flat$ | $\mid G^{ø7}$ $C^7$) | $\mid F\text{MI}^7$ | $\mid (E\flat\text{MI}^7$ $A\flat^7)$ $\mid$ |
| 5 | 6 | 7 | 8 |
| $\mid D\flat^9$ | $\mid (G^{ø7})$ $C_{\text{ALT}}$ | $\mid F\text{MI}^7$ ($D^{ø7}$ | $\mid G^{ø7}$ $C^{7(\flat9)})$ $\mid$ |
| 9 | 10 | 11 | 12 |

**Diagram 18. 1   12-bar minor blues (with optional chords)**

## Exercises

1.  Notate chord symbols and melodies for the progression below in the keys of: C minor, F minor, and E♭ minor.  Practice improvisation as well.

*(T.A. to VI)*    *(T.A. to iv)*    *(T.A. to III)*

| iMI$^6$ | viiMI$^7$-III$^7$ | VIMA$^7$ | vMI$^7$-I$^7$ | iv$^7$ | iv$^7$-VII$^7$ | IIIMA$^7$ | ii$^{ø7}$-V$^7$ | iMI$^6$ |

2.  Notate the chord symbols to the turnback and ground bass progressions in the keys of D minor, G minor, and A minor; each chord is two beats in duration.  Practice improvising to an alternation between these two progressions.
3.  Compose melodies and practice improvisation to the "Whisper Not" progression as it appears in Example 18.7, using the keys of C minor, E minor, and G minor [Note: begin on the subtonic chord and end on tonic].
4.  Practice improvising to the tune *Mr. Funk*, using principles discussed in this chapter.  Be sure to analyze the harmonic idioms, noting the "curve" in the progression.  Be prepared to ascertain methods of negotiating this "curve" in the changes.

# Mr. Funk

SEE APPENDIX 1 FOR B♭, E♭, AND
BASS CLEF TRANSPOSITIONS

CHAPTER 19

# Blues Revisited
### "Cycle Blues"

## Blues Progressions

There are many variations to the 12-bar blues progression, allowing the proficient improviser an opportunity to alter the progression with each successive chorus. The possibilities for variation can best be studied by dividing the blues into three 4-bar phrases.

**Part 1: Measures 1-4** • The first phrase of the blues establishes tonic and concludes with a turnaround to the IV chord in measure 5. The possibilities for variation are as follows:
1. The tonic chord in measures 1 and 3 can be either a dominant seventh or a major seventh, allowing for the solo to be either bluesy or progressive sounding.
2. A $\sharp$IV$^{o7}$ can be added to the last half of measure 2 (as was described in Chapter 13).
3. Measure 4 can contain either a I$^7$ chord or a complete turnaround to IV (VMI$^7$-I$^7$, see Chapter 10).

Diagram 19.1 displays the harmonic possibilities for Part 1 of the 12-bar blues, using both Roman numerals and the chord symbols for the key of F.

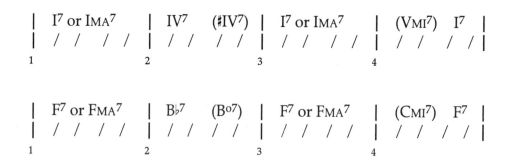

**Diagram 19.1    Part 1 (mm. 1-4) of the 12-bar blues**

Example 19.1 shows a melody making use of the substitute possibilities for the first four bars of the blues.

**Ex. 19.1   Melody for mm. 1-4 of 12 bar blues**

**Part 2: Measures 5-8** • The second section of the 12-bar blues can be seen as a juxtaposition of the IV-to-I progression (Chapters 13-15) and the I-to-VI$^7$ progression (Chapter 16), so obviously a great many substitute possibilities exist.  They can be outlined as follows:

1. From measure 5 to the downbeat of measure 7 is the IV-I progression, with measure 5 being entirely occupied by the IV chord (which can be major 7th or dominant 7th).
2. Measure 6 features the connecting chord(s) between IV and I, which could be ♯iv$^{o7}$ or ivMI$^7$ (or MI$^6$).  Remember that a ♭VII$^7$ can be used after ivMI$^7$, creating the deceptive resolution to tonic.

Diagram 19.2 outlines the choices for measures 5 and 6.

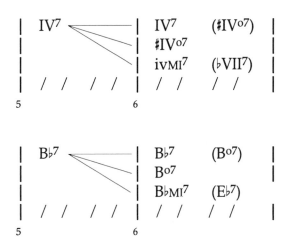

**Diagram 19.2   Part 2 (mm. 5-6) of the 12-bar blues**

Example 19.2 contains melodies which make use of the substitute possibilities in measures 5 and 6 of the 12-bar blues.

**Ex. 19.2   Melody for mm. 5-6 of 12 bar blues**

3. Measure 7 typically begins with the tonic chord which initiates the I-VI$^7$ progression (refer to Chapter 16 for a discussion of all the substitute chord choices).
4. Measure 7 also can begin with a iii$^7$ or iii$^{\o7}$ chord (although it will *not* follow ♯iv$^{o7}$).  In this case, measure 8 will consist entirely of the VI$^7$ chord, which leads in the circle of fifths to ii$^7$ in bar 9.
5. When measure 7 begins on iii$^7$, one substitution is reasonably employed.  In this instance, the iii-VI progression will take place entirely in measure 7, followed by the same chords down a half step in measure 8 (♭iii-♭VI, as seen in Chapter 16).  This type of substitution often follows ♭VII$^7$.

Diagram 19.3 displays the progressions for measures 7 and 8 of a 12-bar blues.

| | | | |
|---|---|---|---|
| I$^7$ or MA$^7$ —— | iii$^7$ | VI$^7$ | |
| I$^7$   VII$^7$ —— | ♭VII$^7$ | VI$^7$ | |
| | | | |
| iii$^7$ —————— | VI$^7$ | | |
| iii$^7$   VI$^7$ —— | ♭iii$^7$ | ♭VI$^7$ | |
| /  /   /  / | /  / | /  / | |

7                                      8

| | | | |
|---|---|---|---|
| F$^7$ or FMA$^7$—— | AMI$^7$ | D$^7$ | |
| F$^7$   E$^7$ —— | E♭$^7$ | D$^7$ | |
| | | | |
| AMI$^7$ (A$^{\o7}$) —— | D$^{7(-9)}$ | | |
| AMI$^7$   D$^7$ —— | A♭MI$^7$ | D♭$^7$ | |
| /  /   /  / | /  / | /  / | |

7                                      8

**Diagram 19.3   Part 2 (mm. 7-8) of the 12-bar blues**

Example 19.3 displays some melodic possibilities for measures 7 and 8 of the 12-bar blues.

**Ex. 19.3   Melodies for  mm. 7-8 of 12 bar blues**

Diagram 19.4 recaps the myriad of possibilities for the entire second phrase of the 12-bar blues.

NOTE: When ♯IVᵒ⁷ progresses to tonic, commonly the bass note is the 5th of the chord (i.e. F/C).

**Diagram 19.4    Part 2 (mm. 5-8) of the 12-bar blues**

**Part 3: Measures 9-12 •** There is very little variety in the final phrase of a 12-bar blues. The function of these measures is to turnaround to a tonic chord at measure 10.  As is the case with most tunes, a turnback progression is usual from mm. 10-12 in order to prepare for the subsequent choruses.  One possible substitution involves replacing I⁷ with iii⁷ at bar 10.  Diagram 19.5 shows the final phrase of blues as it is typically played.

```
|  ii⁷        |  V⁷ ――――  |  I⁷   (VI⁷  |  ii⁷    V⁷) |
|             |           |  iii⁷ ―      |             |
| / / / /   | / / / /   | / / / /   | / / / / |
 9            10           11     12
```

```
|  Gᴍɪ⁷       |  C⁷ ――――  |  F⁷   (D⁷   |  Gᴍɪ⁷   C⁷) |
|             |           |  Aᴍɪ⁷ ―      |             |
| / / / /   | / / / /   | / / / /   | / / / / |
 9            10           11     12
```

**Diagram 19.5   Part 3  (final phrase, mm. 9-12) of the 12-bar blues**

Diagram 19.6 assembles the entire flow chart for the 12-bar blues progression.

```
|  I⁷ or Iᴍᴀ⁷ |  IV⁷    (♯IV⁷) |  I⁷ or Iᴍᴀ⁷ |  (Vᴍɪ⁷)  I⁷ |
| / / / /   | / /    / /    | / / / /   | / /  / / |
 1            2               3            4
```

```
|  IV⁷ or IVᴍᴀ⁷― |  IV⁷  (♯IVᵒ⁷)― |  I⁷ or Iᴍᴀ⁷ ―― |  iii⁷    VI⁷ |
|                |  ♯IVᵒ⁷          |  I⁷   VII⁷ ―― |  ♭VII⁷   VI⁷ |
|                |                |                |             |
|                |                |  iii ―――――― |  VI⁷        |
|                |  IVᴍɪ⁷  (♭VII⁷)― |  iii⁷   VI ― |  ♭iii⁷   ♭VI⁷ |
| / / / /      | / /   / /     | / / / /      | / /   / / |
 5               6                7               8
```

```
|  ii⁷        |  V⁷ ――――  |  I⁷   (VI⁷  |  ii⁷    V⁷) |
|             |           |  iii⁷ ―      |             |
| / / / /   | / / / /   | / / / /   | / / / / |
 9            10           11     12
```

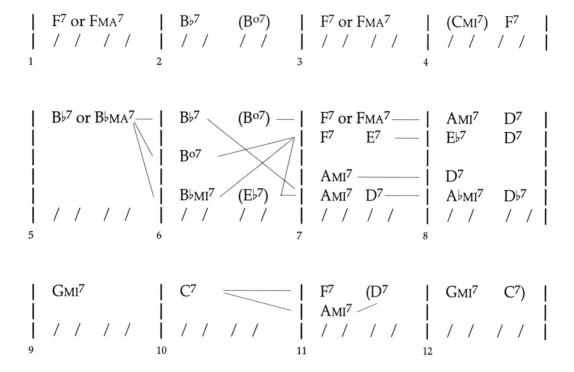

**Diagram 19.6   The Blues Flow Chart**

## Cycle or Circle Blues

A popular progression based on the 12-bar blues is the *cycle* or *circle* blues, so named for its usage of the circle of fifths. This format is also called "Bird Blues," with respect to alto saxophonist Charlie "Yardbird" Parker. There are a few variations to this progression, which features a succession of descending ii-V turnarounds. The cycle blues is related to the more traditional blues in that both progressions begin on tonic, turnaround to IV at measure 5, and return to tonic at the end. Diagram 19.7 on the following page depicts a cycle blues progression.

| $I_{MA}^7$ | | $vii^{ø7}$ $III^7$ | | $vi_{MI}^7$ $II^7$ | | $v_{MI}^7$ $I^7$ |
|---|---|---|---|---|---|---|
| / / / / | | / / / / | | / / / / | | / / / / |
| 1 | | 2 | | 3 | | 4 |

| $IV_{MA}^7$ | | $iv_{MI}^7$ $\flat VII^7$ | $iii_{MI}^7$ $VI^7$ | | $\flat iii^7$ $\flat VI^7$ |
|---|---|---|---|---|---|
| | | | $\flat III_{MA}^7$ | | |
| / / / / | | / / / / | / / / / | | / / / / |
| 5 | | 6 | 7 | | 8 |

| $ii_{MI}^7$ | | $V^7$ | | $iii^7$ $VI^7$ | | $ii^7$ $V^7$ |
|---|---|---|---|---|---|---|
| | | $iv_{MI}^7$ $bVII^7$ | | | | |
| / / / / | | / / / / | | / / / / | | / / / / |
| 9 | | 10 | | 11 | | 12 |

| $F_{MA}^7$ | | $E^{ø7}$ $A^7$ | | $D_{MI}^7$ $G^7$ | | $C_{MI}^7$ $F^7$ |
|---|---|---|---|---|---|---|
| / / / / | | / / / / | | / / / / | | / / / / |
| 1 | | 2 | | 3 | | 4 |

| $B\flat_{MA}^7$ | | $B\flat_{MI}^7$ $E\flat^7$ | $A_{MI}^7$ $D^7$ | | $A\flat_{MI}^7$ $D\flat^7$ |
|---|---|---|---|---|---|
| | | | $A\flat_{MA}^7$ | | |
| / / / / | | / / / / | / / / / | | / / / / |
| 5 | | 6 | 7 | | 8 |

| $G_{MI}^7$ | | $C^7$ | | $A_{MI}^7$ $D^7$ | | $G_{MI}^7$ $C^7$ |
|---|---|---|---|---|---|---|
| | | $B\flat_{MI}^7$ $E\flat^7$ | | | | |
| / / / / | | / / / / | | / / / / | | / / / / |
| 9 | | 10 | | 11 | | 12 |

**Diagram 19.7    Cycle Blues**

## Exercises

1. Diagram six different progressions for measures 5-8 of a 12-bar blues in the key of F.
2. Transpose the progressions above to C, B♭, D♭, and G.
3. Compose melody lines for three of your progressions above.
4. Prepare to improvise to the song *Lots More Blues* in class, using the various substitute progressions outlined in this chapter.
5. Prepare to improvise to the tune *Cycles*.
6. Transcribe a solo to a 12-bar blues progression, analyzing the substitute progressions employed by the performer.

7. Bring recordings of blues performances into class, for aural recognition of substitute progressions.
8. Prepare a Roman numeral analysis for the progressions of *Lots More Blues* and *Cycles*.
9. Analyze the sample solos to *Lots More Blues* and *Cycles* (Appendix 2), identifying characteristic jazz formulae and usage of substitute idioms.

*Lots More Blues*

SEE APPENDIX 1 FOR B♭, E♭, AND
BASS CLEF TRANSPOSITIONS

*Cycles*

SEE APPENDIX 1 FOR B♭, E♭, AND
BASS CLEF TRANSPOSITIONS

CHAPTER 20

# Substitute Harmonic Idioms

As was discussed in Chapter 18 chords in major keys are more chromatic and less bluesy than those in minor, giving rise to a more sophisticated style of improvisation. There are many *substitute harmonic idioms* that mature improvisers superimose over standard chord changes in major keys. It is possible for a seasoned improviser to use substitute harmony to subtly vary the changes for each chorus of a solo (as was demonstrated over blues in Chapter 19).

The substitute harmonic idioms discussed so far include:
1.  ii-chord substitution (Chapter 14)
2.  tritone substitution - functional and passing (Chapter 15)
3.  IV to I progressions - three interchangeable progressions (Chapter 13-15)
4.  I to VI progressions -there are six basic I-VI progressions, augmented by adding tritone substitution (Chapter 16)
5.  diminished substitutions - ♭iii°7 for VI (iii-♭iii°-ii-V), ♯I°7 for VI (I-♯I°7-ii-V) (Chapter 13)

There are other substitute harmonic idioms typical to jazz improvisation, which are listed below and will be explained in this chapter:
6.  turnaround up a half step - often used at phrase endings to precede ii-V
7.  the tritone substituted ("Bill Evans") turnaround - uses tritone substitution for both the ii and V chords of a turnaround progression
8.  auxiliary chords - provide tension and release by delaying the anticipated harmony
9.  the "Coltrane" turnback - substitutes changes from the *Giant Steps* progression

**Turnaround Up a Half Step** • Often employed at phrase endings, a complete ii-V turnaround, up a half step from ii-V in the key, affords an almost entirely new set of pitches for improvisation. This harmonic device can be used when the structure of the song allows one measure each for the ii and V chords. The substitution involves playing each chord of the new progression for two beats, as displayed in Example. 20.1.

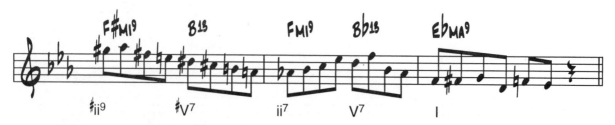

**Ex. 20.1  Turnaround up 1/2 step**

[Note: The turnaround up a half step is most effective when the melody of the song features the 3rd of the ii chord because that pitch is found in each chord of the new progression. For example, in the key of E♭ major, the note A♭ is the 3rd of the ii chord (Fᴍɪ⁷) and 7th of V⁷ (B♭⁷), but is also the 9th of the raised ii chord (F♯ᴍɪ⁷) and the 13th of the raised V⁷ (B⁷).]

**Tritone Substituted ("Bill Evans") Turnaround** • This substitute possibility was used frequently and to great effect by the pianist, Bill Evans. The *tritone substituted turnaround* occurs entirely over the V chord of a ii-V-I progression. In place of the V⁷ chord is inserted tritone-substituted chords for both ii and V. For example, ii-V-I in C major is |Dᴍɪ⁷|G⁷|Cᴍᴀ⁷|, while the "Bill Evans" turnaround would be |Dᴍɪ⁷|A♭ᴍɪ⁷-D♭⁹|Cᴍᴀ⁷|. Example 20.2 depicts a melody over the "Bill Evans" turnaround.

Ex. 20.2 The "Bill Evans" (tritone substitute) turnaround

In songs utilizing successive chords in the circle of fifths, two or more "Bill Evans" turnarounds can be "chained" together. Example 20.3 exhibits a chain of tritone substituted turnarounds for the progression in *Get Out the Rake*.

Ex. 20.3 Chain of tritone substitute turnarounds

It should be noted that the improviser can execute the above substitutions whether or not they are being played by the rhythm section. Because these progressions resolve to tonics, their logic is not obscured by the basic chord changes, but rather the new progressions sound pleasingly "outside."

**Auxiliary Chords** • Chapter 18 shows the subdominant chord as an auxiliary harmony to tonic, but other auxiliary sonorities are posible. An improviser sounds the auxiliary sonority at the point of resolution to a tonic, thereby delaying the expected resolution and adding to the tension/release dynamics of the solo.

Auxiliary chords contain a common tone to the embellished tonic (most often the root), and other notes of the auxiliary chord resolve stepwise into tones of the tonic harmony. Diminished 7th chords are effective as auxiliary sonorities, as shown in Example 20.4.

**Ex. 20.4   Auxiliary °7 chord**

Example 20.5 illustrates other examples of chords which can serve in an auxiliary fashion (auxiliary chords are bracketed).

**Ex. 20.5   Other auxiliary chords**

**The "Coltrane" Turnback** • In the 1960's, tenor saxophonist John Coltrane was at the forefront of a movement to revolutionize jazz harmony. His tune *Giant Steps* explored chord progressions departing from circle-of-fifths relationships. *Giant Steps* is characterized by root motion up a minor 3rd from tonic, and then ascending a perfect 4th from the second chord. The "Coltrane" turnback begins on tonic, progresses up a minor 3rd, then a perfect 4th, before resolving down by half step into V$^7$, as shown in Example 20.6.

**Ex. 20.6  The "Coltrane" turnback**

[Note: In the Coltrane turnback, the ♭VI⁷ can also be a MA⁷ chord. Also a tritone substitution for V⁷ is possible. So the progression above could also be played C⁶-E♭⁹-A♭MA⁹-G⁷⁽♭⁹⁾-CMA⁹, or C⁶-E♭⁹-A♭MA⁹-D♭⁹ (or D♭MA⁹)-CMA⁹.]

The pentatonic and quartal improvisational techniques discussed in Chapters 21 and 22 can be used effectively over non-traditional chord progressions such as those found in *Giant Steps*.

**Exercises**

1. Practice the turnaround-up-a-half-step progression, as depicted in Example 20.1 in the keys of: F major, B♭ major, E♭ major, A♭ major, and G major.
2. Compose melodies and improvise to the "Bill Evans" turnaround in the keys of Exercise 1.
3. Notate five auxiliary chords to each of the following sonorities, and practice improvising those chords and their resolutions: C major, E♭ major, and D major.
4. Notate the chord symbols and practice the "Coltrane" turnback in all major keys.
5. Bring a standard song into class, with substitute harmony progressions indicated above the staff, and improvise using the substitute harmony.

CHAPTER 21

# Polyharmony
## (Superimposed Triads)

### Pentatonic Scales, II Dominant Idioms, The "Diminished Domain"

## Polyharmony

In classical music, *polyharmony* (or polytonality) refers to sounding two different chords at once. In jazz, it can better be described as improvising to a different triad than the prevailing chord (*superimposed triad*).. Polyharmonic (superimposed) playing is made possible by the fact that the extended chords used in jazz contain other triads. For instance, every major ninth chord also contains a minor seventh chord built on the 3rd, and another major triad constructed from the 5th. Example 21.1 shows the "other" chords contained within a CMA$^9$ chord.

**Ex. 21.1  Major ninth chord and other chords contained within**

The possibilities for polyharmony increase as altered extensions are considered. This chapter will concentrate on the most consonant ("inside") polyharmonic major triads, with an understanding that the relative minor triads can also be used (i.e. if C major is a viable polychord, then its relative minor, A minor, may also be played).

**Major Ninth Chords** • There are two consonant polychords for major ninth harmony. They are:
1. the major triad up a perfect fifth (as seen in Example 21.1).
2. the major triad up a whole step. This chord contains a #11 (or ♭5th) which is a consonant note in jazz.

Example 21.1 displays a major ninth chord and its coincident polychords.

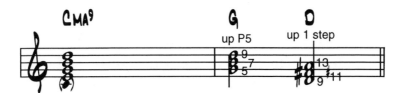

**Ex.21.2  Poytonal triads for MA⁹ chord**

It should be noted that the improviser can isolate the superimposed triad, or incorporate it within a line emphasizing basic chord tones.  Example 21.3 demonstrates both approaches.

**Ex. 21.3  Polyharmony isolated and incorporated into the chord change**

**Minor Ninth Chords** • There are three feasible polychords for minor ninth harmony. They are:
1.  the major triad up a minor third (this is the relative major).
2.  the major triad down a whole step.  This chord contains a consonant 11th and is the most frequent choice of improvisers.
3.  the major triad up a perfect fourth, provided the minor seventh is functioning as ii⁷, then this chord is the accompanying V.

Example 21.4 displays the polychords for minor ninth harmony.

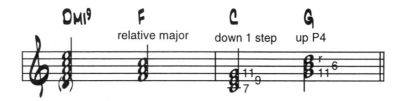

**Ex. 21.4  Polytonal triads for MI⁹ chords**

**Half-Diminished Chords** • The possibilities for polyharmony are more vague with regards to half-diminished chords, and the usage is linked to the resolution of the half-diminished sonority. Unlike the polychords above, those used with half-diminished chords are not entirely consonant. The most consonant polychords are:

1.  the major triad down a whole step. This is the most widely-used choice.
2.  the major triad down a major third. This chord is also best suited to connecting with altered dominants.
3.  the major triad a tritone away. This sound is most effective when the half-diminished chord progresses to an altered dominant.

Example 21.5 displays the polyharmonies for half-diminished chords.

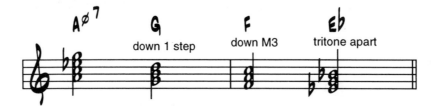

**Ex. 21.5  Polytonal triads for half diminished chords**

**Dominant Chords** • There are no fewer than five possible polytonal triads for dominant harmony, yielding a variety of extended sounds. They are:

1.  the major triad up a whole step, containing the 13th and #11th.
2.  three major triads up successive minor thirds from the chord root (see "Diminished Domain" below):
    a.  the chord up a minor third from the root contains a #9th.
    b.  the next minor third up is the tritone-substitute chord, and highlights the ♭9th and ♭5th.
    c.  the last minor third up yields a triad built on the 13th, which also contains a ♭9th.
3.  the major triad down a major third. This chord accentuates the ♭13th and the #9th (alt.).

Example 21.6 outlines the five polytonal triads for dominant harmony.

**Ex. 21.6  Polytonal triads for dominant harmony**

Example 21.7 depicts a melody which makes use of superimposed sonorities over a dominant chord.

**Ex. 21.7  Melody of superimposed triads over dominant harmony**

## The Diminished Domain

*The Diminished Domain* refers to a world of harmonic possibilities residing within the diminished scale.  As seen in Example 21.8, one diminished scale contains four major (or dominant 7th) chords and four minor (or minor 7th) chords.

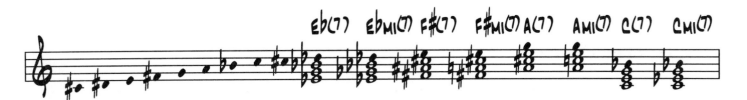

**Ex. 21.8  Eight triads (7th chords) in the diminished scale**

The four dominant chords can be said to "share" a common diminished scale which, along with the eight concurrent triads (7th chords), can be employed for varied and sophisticated improvisation.  Because of the symmetry of the diminished scale, any melody in the Diminished Domain will work for all four dominant chords "sharing" the common diminished scale.  Example 21.9 shows a melody utilizing various super-imposed harmonies from the Diminished Domain and indicating the four dominant chords which can employ that melody.

**Ex. 21.9  "Diminished Domain" melody**

A frequently-used improvisational device involves a combination of parallel major and minor triads (i.e. C major and C minor) in the Diminished Domain, as exemplified by Example 21.10.

**Ex. 21.10   Combination major/minor diminished patterns**

The Diminished Domain affords a wealth of possibilities for polyharmonic improvisation, and as such is a significant component of mature improvisation.

## Pentatonic Scale

A pentatonic scale is any scale consisting of five notes.  In jazz music, *the* pentatonic scale is analogous to a major scale with tones 4 and 7 deleted.  The tones of the pentatonic scale can also be aligned to form a major six-nine chord.  The minor pentatonic scale uses the tones of its relative major (i.e. the pentatonic scales for C major and A minor are the same).  Example 21.11 depicts the C pentatonic scale and its alignment as a six-nine chord.

**Ex. 21.11   Pentatonic scale and six-nine chord**

**Improvisation** • The pentatonic scale is an effective source for melodic invention with polytonal (superimposed) triads.  The usage of the pentatonic scale is "safe" in that it basically highlights the polychord without using many other pitches which may be too dissonant.  The pentatonic scale can be played with any of its notes on the bottom, giving rise to five "modes" of the scale.  Example 21.12 displays the five modes of a pentatonic scale.

**Ex. 21.12   Five modes of the pentatonic scale**

It is also common to use the modes of the scale in four-note groupings, as seen in Example 21.13.

**Ex. 21.13  4-note groupings of pentatonic modes**

By combining polytonal triads through the use of their pentatonic scales, the improviser can create a fresh sound with well-placed chordal extensions.  Example 21.14 displays a melody line employing polytonal pentatonic scales.

**Ex. 21.14  Jazz melody using polytonal pentatonic scales**

The pentatonic style of improvising gives rise to phrases in four-note groupings and regular patterns of accent, and represents a substantive departure from be-bop characteristics.  This type of improvisation is favored by contemporary artists such as Michael Brecker, Freddie Hubbard and Chick Corea.

The four-note groupings can be masked by beginning off the beat, which displaces the regular accent patterns (see Example 21.15).

**Ex. 21.15  Rhythmic displacement of pentatonic pattern**

Variety can also be achieved through employing eighth-note patterns in groupings of six notes (see Example 21.16).

**Ex. 21.16  Six note pentatonic patterns**

Pentatonic improvisation goes hand in hand with "quartal" jazz, which will be discussed in the next chapter.

## II Dominant Idioms

The dominant chord built on supertonic is a frequent component to jazz progressions and almost always precedes ii-V (it is used in seven songs from this book, such as *Mellotones, Catch a Caboose*, etc.). It is traditional for the supertonic dominant to be played with a ♯11th (i.e. $C^7$ would contain F♯). Therefore, the polytonal triad up a step is applicable to the dominant chord built on II. Example 21.17 notates this polychord for a supertonic dominant.

**Ex. 21.17  Polyharmony for II dominant**

Another way to highlight the ♯11th is through ii-chord substitution (see Chapter 14). By using the ascending melodic minor scale of the ii-chord substitute, the ♯11 is also achieved. For instance, if $D^7$ is the supertonic dominant, then its ii-chord substitute is $A_{MI}^7$, and the A ascending melodic minor scale will contain the ♯11th. Example 21.18 outlines the usage of ii-chord substitution and ascending melodic minor scale for supertonic dominant harmony.

**Ex. 21.18  ii chord  sub. and ascending melodic minor**

## Exercises

1.  Notate the polytonal (superimposed) triads for the following major ninth chords: A♭, D, F, C♯.
2.  Notate the polytonal (superimposed) triads for the following minor ninth chords: C, E♭, G, G♯.
3.  Notate the polytonal (superimposed) triads for the following half-diminished chords: A, E, B♭, F♯.
4.  Notate the polytonal (superimposed) triads for the following dominant chords: F, D♭, G, A♭.
5.  Notate the three diminished scales and the eight triads (7th chords) contained within each, circling the dominant seventh chords which "share" each diminished scale.
6.  Compose Diminished Domain melodies for all three diminished scales and indicate the four applicable dominant chords for each.
7.  Notate the pentatonic scales and their modes for the polytonal triads above.
8.  Construct polyharmonic melodies to some of the chords above, as indicated by the instructor.
9.  Prepare to improvise to the tune *Song for a Chick*, using polyharmony and pentatonic scales.
10.  Prepare to improvise to the song *Watch It*, empolying the II-dominant idioms outlined in this chapter.
11.  Analyze the sample solos to *Song for a Chick* and *Watch It* (Appendix 2), identifying characteristic jazz formulae, polyharmonic devices, and the II-dominant idiom.

# *Song for a Chick*

SEE APPENDIX 1 FOR B♭, E♭, AND
BASS CLEF TRANSPOSITIONS

# *Watch It*

SEE APPENDIX 1 FOR B♭, E♭, AND BASS CLEF TRANSPOSITIONS

CHAPTER 22

# Modal Jazz and Quartal Jazz

## Suspended Chords

### Diatonic Modes

The diatonic (church) modes can be described as scales which begin and end on the various notes of the major scale. Each note of the major scale has a mode based upon it. The diatonic modes are as follows:

1. Ionian is the mode name for the major scale itself, and thus is not applicable to jazz.
2. Dorian is the mode beginning on scale degree ii (supertonic).
3. Phrygian is the mode beginning on scale degree iii (mediant).
4. Lydian is the mode beginning on scale degree IV (subdominant).
5. Mixolydian is the mode beginning on scale degree V (dominant).
6. Aeolian is the mode beginning on scale degree vi (submediant).
7. Locrian is the mode beginning on scale degree vii (leading tone). The Locrian mode is not one of the original church modes, but has been added by twentieth century theorists.

Example 22.1 displays the modes derived from the G major scale.

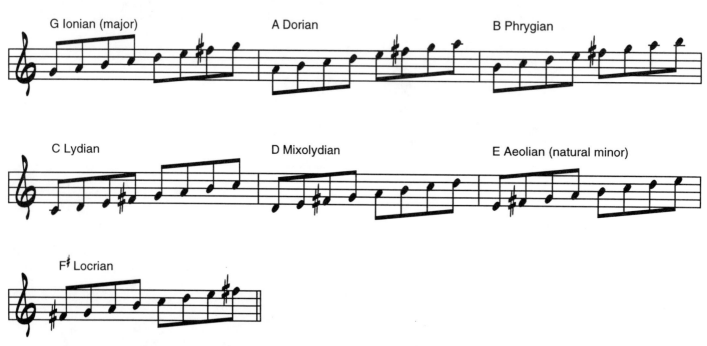

**Ex. 22.1  The diatonic modes, based on G major**

### Characteristics of the Modes

MAJOR • Lydian and Mixolydian are the major-sounding modes because their tonic triads are major chords. Their characteristics are as follows:
1. Lydian sounds like major with a raised fourth scale degree. This mode is very popular with improvisers for major chords, due to the fact that the diatonic 4th is not consonant while the *raised* (Lydian) 4th is.
2. Mixolydian sounds like major with a lowered seventh scale degree. The scale advised in Chapter 5 for dominant harmony can also be described as a Mixolydian scale.

Example 22.2 shows the use of the Lydian 4th in a jazz melody.

**Ex. 22.2  Melody with Lydian 4th**

MINOR • Dorian, Phrygian, and Aeolian are the minor-sounding modes because their tonic triads are minor chords. Their modal characteristics are as follows:
1. Dorian sounds like natural minor with a raised sixth scale degree. The scale advised for ii$^7$ chords in Chapter 6 can also be described as Dorian.
2. Phrygian sounds like natural minor with a lowered second scale degree.
3. Aeolian *is* natural minor, without including the leading tone associated with turnarounds to minor tonics.

The Locrian mode contains a diminished tonic triad. It is not usually applicable to jazz, although the scale prescribed in Chapter 11 for half-diminished ii$^7$ chords can be described as Locrian.

## Modal Jazz

In the late 1950's, some jazz composers began using modes as an alternative to tonal harmony. That is, some jazz tunes are based upon one or more modes instead of functional chord progressions. These tunes tend to have few chords (perhaps only two), with each chord lasting several measures or more. By far the most commonly used mode for this purpose is Dorian, with Phrygian a distant second. *So What* by Miles Davis is a typical example of a Dorian composition, as well as John Coltrane's *Impressions*.

**Improvisation** • The procedures concerning improvisation to modal jazz tunes are as follows:

1. Accentuate the characteristic of the mode (i.e. the note which differentiates it from major or minor).
2. Use the various chords contained within the mode, not just the tonic triad.
3. Use decorative chromaticism for variety. All twelve tones are possible, just as in tonal jazz.
4. Transpose the entire mode for dissonance, and then resolve back to it (this is referred to "outside" playing and will be discussed in Chapter 23). The most frequent transposition is up a half step.
5. Use consonant pentatonic scales, creating melodies based on fourths rather than thirds (see below).
6. Approach a Dorian tonic as if it is a ii chord, and utilize tonal ii-V lines. Likewise, Mixolydian can be viewed as a dominant and treated the same way.

Example 22.3 demonstrates the principle of accentuating modal characteristics.

**Ex. 22.3  Accentuating modal characteristics**

Example 22.4 shows a melody which uses the various chords of the mode.

**Ex. 22.4  Using the chords of the mode**

Example 22.5 demonstrates the "outside" effect of transposing the mode up a half step and resolving back in.

**Ex. 22.5  "Outside" playing, using transposed modes**

## Quartal Jazz

The advent of modal jazz precipitated the technique of *quartal jazz* (i.e. lines based on fourths rather than thirds). The pentatonic scale is usually the source for quartal ideas, in that the tones of the scale can be realigned in perfect 4ths. Example 22.6 shows the notes of the pentatonic scale in their quartal alignment.

**Ex. 22.6   Pentatonic scale and quartal alignment**

By transposing one note up or down an octave in a set of 4ths, several quartal melodic cells can be created from the pentatonic scale. These *quartal cells* characteristically contain three or more of the following intervals: P4, P5, M2, and m7. Example 22.7 depicts some quartal cells and their usage in melody.

**Ex. 22.7   Quartal cells and melodies from pentatonic scale**

The consonant pentatonic scales for the modes are the ones based on the scale degrees which produce major triads (for instance, D Dorian contains major triads on C, F and G, so these are the consonant pentatonic scales). Example 22.8 shows the D Dorian scale and the resultant major triads.

**Ex. 22.8   Dorian scale  and major chords contained within**

The consonant pentatonic scales for the modes used in jazz are as follows:
1. Dorian uses pentatonic scales from the 3rd, 4th, and 7th scale degrees.
2. Phrygian uses pentatonic scales from the 2nd, 3rd, and 6th scale degrees.
3. Lydian uses pentatonic scales from the 1st, 2nd, and 5th scale degrees.
4. Mixolydian uses pentatonic scales from the 1st, 4th, and 7th scale degrees.

5. Aeolian uses pentatonic scales from the 3rd, 6th, and 7th scale degrees.

It should be noted that the quartal palette for improvisation is very effective when used with superimposed triads (as outlined in Chapter 21). The sample solo to *Modal Magic* (Appendix 2) demonstrates the various techniques outlined in this chapter.

## Suspended Chords

In most styles of music (including much of jazz), the interval of a perfect 4th above a root is considered dissonant and requires resolution to a 3rd. This 4th is *suspended* above the 3rd. For minor 7th chords in jazz and in the modal context, the fourth is a consonant tone. When the 4th replaces the 3rd of a chord, a quartal sonority results which is called the *suspended (sus)* or *suspended 7th (sus⁷)* chord. The Dsus and Dsus⁷ chords of Example 22.9 are actually quartal cells from the C pentatonic scale.

**Ex. 22.9  Sus. and sus.⁷ chords**

## Exercises

1. Notate Dorian scales on C, E, and F♯, and circle the note for each which characterizes the mode.
2. Notate Phrygian scales on B, G, and D♯, and circle the note for each which characterizes the mode.
3. Notate Lydian scales on F, A♭, and C, and circle the note for each which characterizes the mode.
4. Notate Mixolydian scales on B♭, A, and E♭, and circle the note for each which characterizes the mode.
5. Take one mode from each exercise above and notate the consonant pentatonic scales.
6. Construct three quartal cells from each pentatonic scale in Exercise 5, and compose a two-measure melody to each scale using the cells.
7. Prepare to improvise to the tune *Modal Magic,* using the techniques outlined in this chapter.
8. Review improvising to *Song for a Chick,* with emphasis on quartal cells within the polytonal (superimposed) harmonies.
9. Bring a recording into class of a modal composition. Analyze the techniques used by the improvisers.
10. Analyze the sample solo to *Modal Magic* (Appendix 2), paying attention to devices described in this chapter.

# *Modal Magic*

SEE APPENDIX 1 FOR B♭, E♭, AND
BASS CLEF TRANSPOSITIONS

CHAPTER 23

# Outside Playing
## All-Purpose Licks, Slash Chords

## Outside Playing

*Outside playing* refers to improvisation which is, at times, highly dissonant and often does not outline the chord changes at all. While some avant-garde players perform consistently in the "outside" realm, more traditional players can use outside techniques effectively. Some procedures for outside playing are as follows:

1.  Use polyharmonies (and their pentatonic scales) which contain one or more dissonant notes. For instance, if the prevailing chord is CMA$^9$, an A major poly-chord will yield one dissonant note (C♯), while a D♭ major polychord will result in a highly dissonant sound. The improviser can determine his own level of dissonance through the choice of polychords.

2.  Use quartal-style playing (see Chapter 22) for the pentatonic scales described above.

3.  Use *parallel chord streams*, that is, playing to chords a prescribed interval from the actual changes. The stream could be a major 3rd away (mildly dissonant), a half step away (sharply dissonant), or any other interval.

4.  Play a characteristic jazz phrase paying *no* attention to the chord tones, or per-haps attempting to emphasize the most dissonant notes against the chord. It is likewise possible to improvise an unrelated progression to the song being played.

5.  Use all-purpose licks (described later in this chapter).

The most effective way to use any of the techniques above is to keep the actual changes in mind and resolve back "inside" to them from time to time.

Example 23.1 depicts the use of dissonant polychords for outside playing.

**Ex. 23.1  "Outside" polyharmony**

Example 23.2 demonstrates the usage of a parallel chord stream against the changes.

**Ex. 23.2   Parallel chord stream**

Example 23.3 displays a jazz line in a characteristic style which is intentionally dissonant against the chord.

**Ex. 23.3   Intentional dissonance**

## All-Purpose Licks

Using chromaticism and sequence, many outside patterns can be created.  These lines work for any chord change and in any key, hence they can be called "all-purpose" licks.

An often-used all-purpose lick involves a descending half step followed by an ascending whole step, as seen in Example 23.4.

**Ex. 23.4   All purpose lick**

Another common all-purpose device uses two descending half steps followed by an ascending skip (of perhaps a major or minor 3rd).  This pattern can descend sequentially by a prescribed interval of a step or a third, as seen in Example 23.5.

**Ex. 23.5   All purpose lick**

An all-purpose lick can be created by chromatically sequencing an interval (2nds, 3rds, and 4ths all work) as shown in Example 23.6.

**Ex. 23.6   All purpose lick**

## Outside Rhythmic Devices (Polyrhythm)

The contemporary improviser stretches the boundaries of rhythm as well as harmony. This can be accomplished in any of several manners. *Polyrhythm* is achieved when the performed rhythm seems to be at odds with the time signature and tempo. Example 23.7 displays a polyrhythmic pattern where each note has the value of two, eighth-note triplet notes (this is a displaced quarter-note triplet figure).

**Ex. 23.7   Displaced quarter note triplet**

Another polyrhythmic device employs an unconventional grouping of a typical rhythm, such as triplets grouped in fours (see Example 23.8).

**Ex. 23.8   Triplets grouped in fours**

*Isorhythm* occurs when a pattern which is not symmetric to the meter recurs against it, as shown in Example 23.9.

**Ex. 23.9   Isorhythmic pattern**

*Asymmetric rhythms* occur when the number of notes within the beat are not symmetric to the meter, such as four-note groupings within a beat of 6/8, or groupings of 5 and 7 notes within a beat of 4/4 (see Example 23.10).

**Ex. 23.10   Asymetric rhythms**

Finally, rhythm can be treated in an entirely free manner analogous to playing outside the harmony. In this context, the improviser is aware of rhythm and tempo, but chooses to remain outside of it, as depicted in Example 23.11.

**Ex. 23.11   "Free" rhythm**

## Slash Chords

*Slash chords* are instances where a chord (usually a triad) occurs over a bass note not found within that chord. The slash chord is indicated by a diagonal line between the name of the chord and the bass note. Improvising is usually simple, relying on the combined notes of the chord and bass, which tend to create an exotic sound. A common slash chord is a major triad over the bass note up one step (i.e. F/G). This sound can be a modal tonic or a pop-sounding V chord (with the bass note indicating the function), as depicted in Example 23.12.

**Ex. 23.12   Slash chord (pop dominant or modal tonic)**

More dissonant slash chords are achieved when the major triad is played over the bass note up a half step or a tritone away.  In either case, the resulting sonority can be used as an outside tonic, or a Diminished Domain dominant, as seen in Example 23.13.

**Ex. 23.13   Slash chords - dominant or "outside" tonic**

An augmented sonority results when a major triad is sounded over the raised 5th (lowered 6th) degree; see Example 23.14.

**Ex. 23.14   Slash chord (augmented tonic sound)**

As with outside playing and rhythmic devices, the possibilities for slash chords are limited only by the imagination of the composer or improviser.

## Improvisation to Non-Traditional Progressions

Of equal importance to playing "outside" is the ability to improvise effectively "inside" non-traditional chord progressions. Beginning in the 1960's, composers such as Wayne Shorter, Herbie Hancock, John Coltrane, and others were exploring progressions characterized by non-circle-of-fifths relationships, and altered major and minor chords (typically #11 for major, 11 for minor, suspended chords, and slash chords).

Some suggestions are offered below for improvisation to non-traditional progressions, with examples derived from the progression to *Far Out*, the tune at the end of this chapter.

1. Emphasize the altered and added notes to chords, as depicted in Example 23.15.

**Ex. 23.15  Emphasizing altered added notes**

2. Define tension and release points in the progression by thinking of the less dissonant sounds as chords of resolution (see Example 23.16).

**Ex. 23.16  Resolution into less dissonant chord**

3. Create melodic resolution (analogous to tendency-tone resolution in circle-of-fifths progressions) by effecting stepwise motion from one chord to the next; see Example 23.17.

**Ex. 23.17  Stepwise melodic resolution**

4. Improvise in a cohesive, motivic fashion, allowing for notes of repetitions of the motive to change to reflect each successive chord. Using this approach, the melody itself is paramount and self-generating, while an awareness of the changing chords allows the improviser to make appropriate adjustments. This style of improvisation is evident in the improvisations of such contemporary guitarists as Pat Metheny, John Scofield, Mike Stern, etc., and is demonstrated in Example 23.18.

**Ex. 23.18   Cohesive motivic melody**

Playing the changes has been compared to traveling down a river. The traditional player negotiates the river in a boat, following its twists and turns, while the outside player soars above, as a bird, occasionally touching down to feel the water.

*     *     *

The past twenty-three chapters have outlined the rich and varied language of contemporary jazz. It is the task of the student through study, practice, and most of all, listening to incorporate these elements into a personal style of improvisation. There are few rewards in art as great as that derived from the spontaneous creation of worthwhile melody. In present-day music, this reward is reserved almost exclusively for the ingenious jazz improviser.

**Exercises**

1. Review songs in this book, exploring the possibilities for outside playing devices.
2. Compose 3 all-purpose patterns.
3. Bring recordings to class for analysis of outside playing.
4. Create a progression using slash chords, as depicted in Examples 23.12-23.14, then compose a solo and improvise to your progression.
5. Prepare to improvise to the tune *Far Out*, using the outside techniques described in this chapter.

## Far Out

SEE APPENDIX 1 FOR B♭, E♭, AND
BASS CLEF TRANSPOSITIONS

# SECTION 5

# Appendices

# APPENDIX 1
# Transposed Tunes

*Bb Part*
## *Majority*

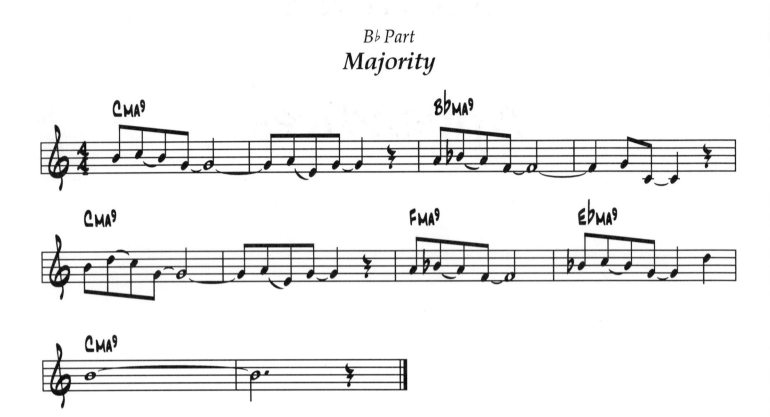

*Eb Part*
## *Majority*

*Bass Clef Part*
## Majority

*B♭ Part*
## Dominant Functions

*E♭ Part*
# Dominant Functions

*Bass Clef Part*
# Dominant Functions

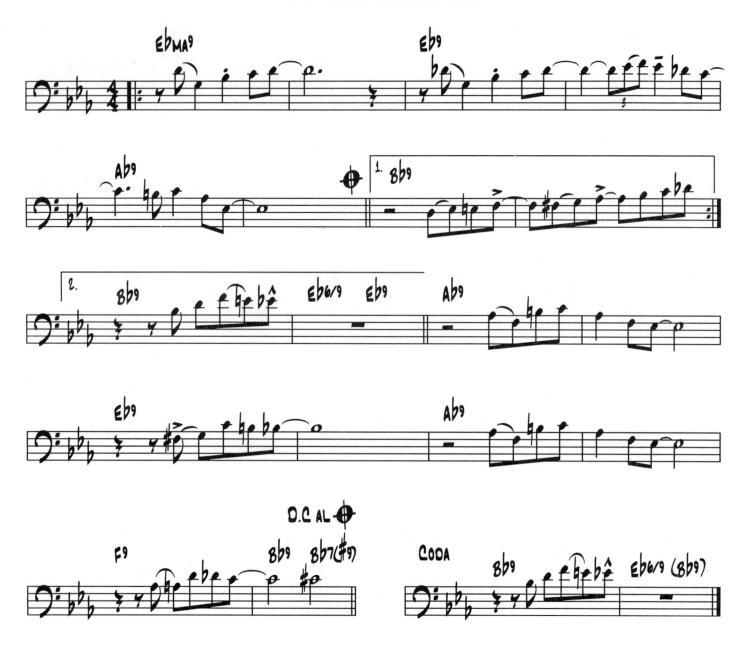

*Bb Part*
# *Minor Difficulties*

**\*Last time after solos**

*Eb Part*
# Minor Difficulties

**\*Last time after solos**

### Bass Clef Part
# *Minor Difficulties*

**\*Last time after solos**

*Bb Part*
## Little "J" Blues

*Eb Part*
## Little "J" Blues

Bass Clef Part
## Little "J" Blues

*Bb Part*
## Mellotones

*E♭ Part*
## *Mellotones*

*Bass Clef Part*
## Mellotones

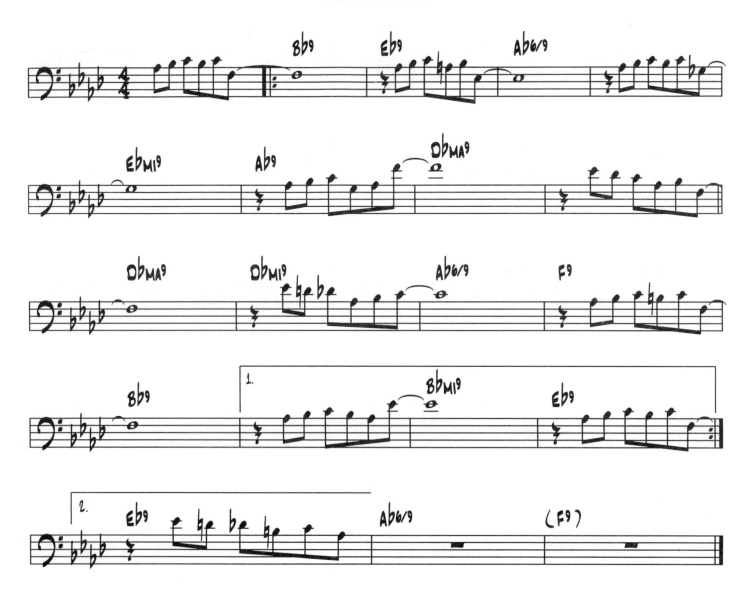

*B♭ Part*
## Catch a Caboose

*Eb Part*
## Catch a Caboose

*Bass Clef Part*
## Catch a Caboose

*Bb Part*
# Lacey Lady

*E♭ Part*
## Lacey Lady

*Bass Clef Part*
## Lacey Lady

*Bb Part*
# Get Out the Rake

Eb Part
# Get Out the Rake

*Bass Clef Part*
## Get Out the Rake

*B♭ Part*
## You Again

*Eb Part*
## You Again

*Bass Clef Part*
## You Again

*Bb Part*
# Grapes and Flowers

*E♭ Part*
## Grapes and Flowers

*Bass Clef Part*
## *Grapes and Flowers*

*Bb Part*
# Parts of You

E♭ *Part*
# *Parts of You*

*Bass Clef Part*
# *Parts of You*

*B♭ Part*
# Rhythm Changes

*E♭ Part*
## Rhythm Changes

*Bass Clef Part*
## Rhythm Changes

*Bb Part*
## Paradoxy

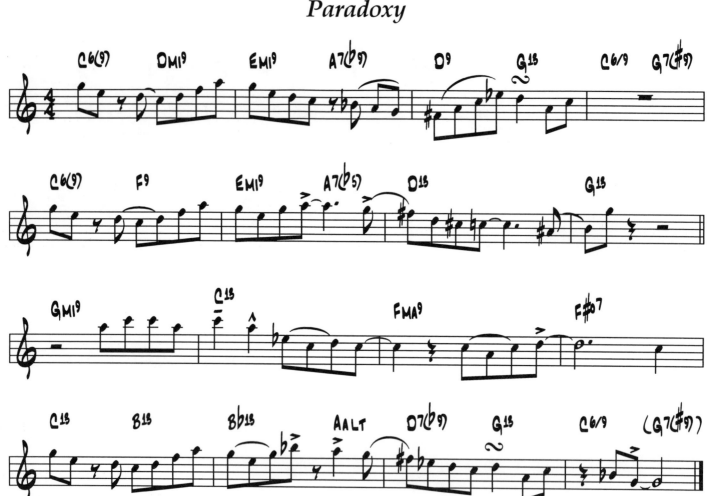

*Eb Part*
## Paradoxy

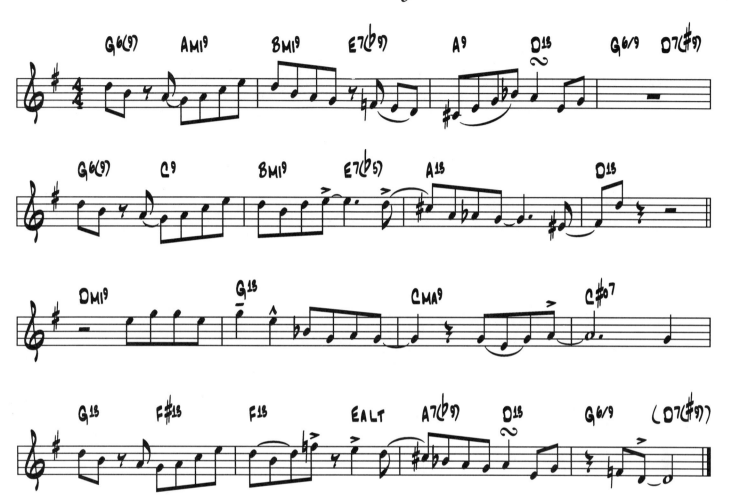

*Bass Clef Part*
## *Paradoxy*

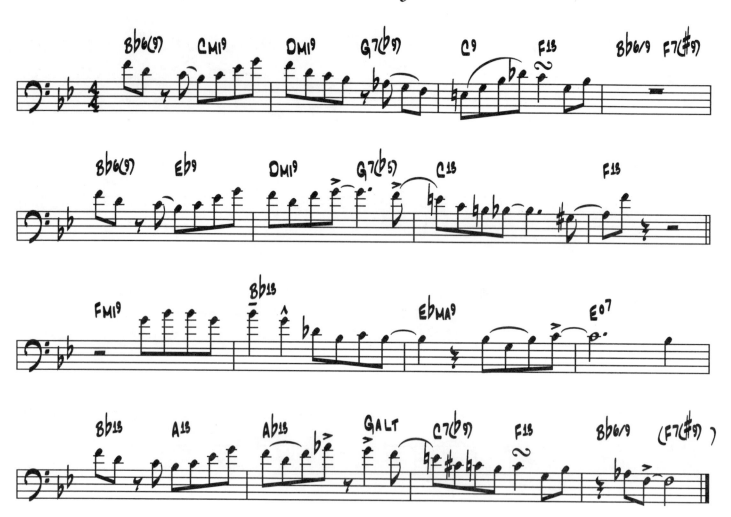

*Bb Part*
# *Tingle*

*E♭ Part*
## Tingle

*Bass Clef Part*
# Tingle

*Bb Part*
## Steps and Circles

*E♭ Part*
## Steps and Circles

*Bass Clef Part*
## Steps and Circles

*B♭ Part*
# Mr. Funk

*Eb Part*
# Mr. Funk

Bass Clef Part
## *Mr. Funk*

*Bb Part*
## Lots More Blues

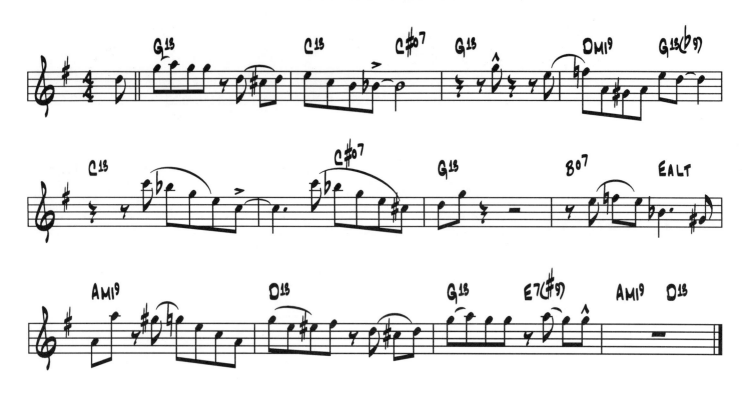

*Eb Part*
## Lots More Blues

*Bass Clef Part*
# Lots More Blues

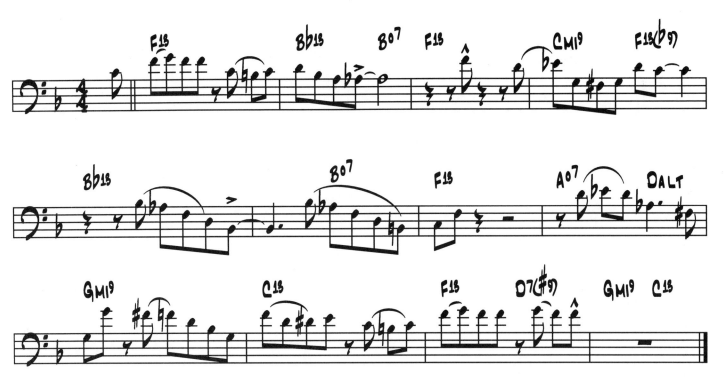

*Bb Part*
# Cycles

*Eb Part*
## Cycles

*Bass Clef Part*
## Cycles

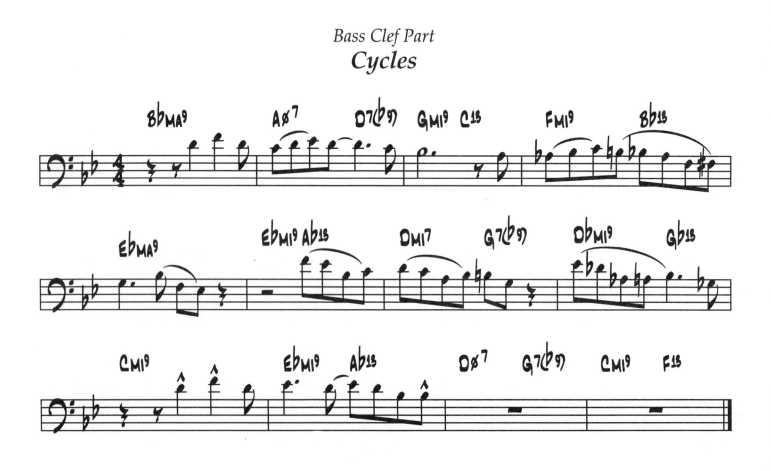

Bb Part
# Song for a Chick

*E♭ Part*
# Song for a Chick

*Bass Clef Part*
# Song for a Chick

*Bb Part*
# Watch It

*E♭ Part*
## Watch It

*Bass Clef Part*
## *Watch It*

*Bb Part*
## *Modal Magic*

*E♭ Part*
## Modal Magic

*Bass Clef Part*
## *Modal Magic*

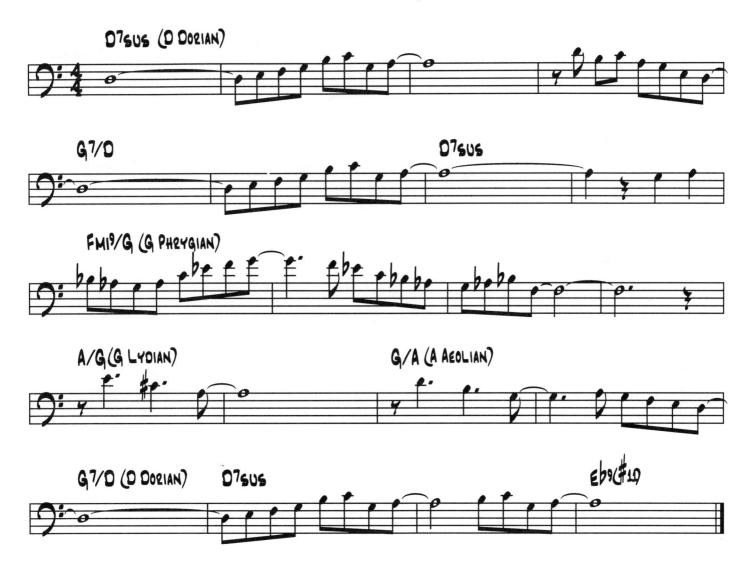

*Bb Part*
# Far Out

*Eb Part*
## *Far Out*

*Bass Clef Part*
## *Far Out*

# APPENDIX 2

# Sample Solos

*Sample Solo*
## *Majority*

*Sample Solo*
# Dominant Functions

*Sample Solo*
## Minor Difficulties

*Sample Solo*
## Little "J" Blues

*Sample Solo*
## Mellotones

*Sample Solo*
## Catch a Caboose

*Sample Solo*
## Lacey Lady

*Sample Solo*
## Get Out the Rake

*Sample Solos*
## You Again

Sample Solo
## Grapes and Flowers

*Sample Solo*
## *Parts of You*

*Sample Solo*
## Rhythm Changes

*Sample Solo*
## Paradoxy

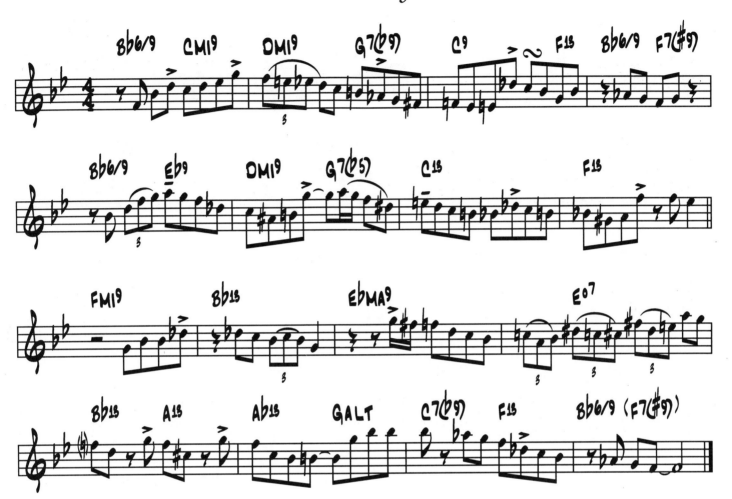

*Sample Solo*
# Tingle

*Sample Solo*
# Steps and Circles

*Sample Solo*
## Mr. Funk

*Sample Solo*
## Lots More Blues

*Sample Solo*
## Cycles

Sample Solo
# Song for a Chick

*Sample Solo*
## Watch It

*Sample Solo*
# Modal Magic

*Sample Solo*
# *Far Out*

APPENDIX 3

# The Circle of Fifths

## The Diatonic Circle of Fifths

The diagram below shows the arrangement of the diatonic chords in a descending circle of fifths (ascending fourths). Each chord in the circle of fifths will resolve to the next, with 7ths resolving to 3rds, 9ths to 5ths, and possibly 13ths to 9ths. These resolutions are down by step. 3rds may remain stationary to become sevenths.

$$I^7 - IV^7 - VII^7 - III^7 - VI^7 - II^7 - V^7 - I^7$$

Any chord in the diatonic circle of fifths can be altered to become a dominant, provided the next chord is a perfect fifth (or ascending fourth) away. This alteration increases the pull towards the next chord and tends to tonicise it.

## The Circle of Fifths (of Key Signatures)

Key signatures relate to each other in the circle of fifths. Each ascending perfect fifth from "C" produces a tonic with one more sharp than the last. Each descending perfect fifth from "C" produces a tonic with one more flat than the last.

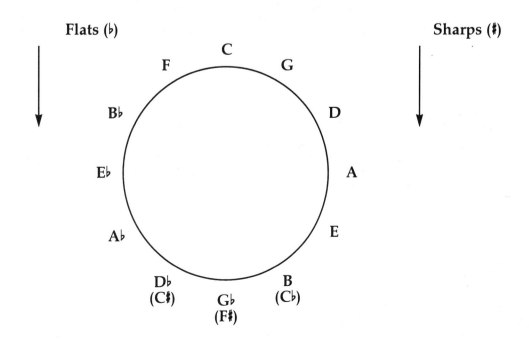

APPENDIX 4

# Scale Preferences

# APPENDIX 5

# Formula Recap

GRACE NOTES: One or several may embellish a chord tone.

MORDANT: Turn employing upper and lower auxiliaries.

BLUE NOTES: Flatted 3rd, 5th, and 7th of the key.

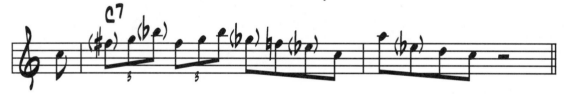

TRIPLET ARPEGGIO: Ascending, begins half step below root or 3rd.

AUXILIARIES: Serve to delay and emphasize a chord tone.

CHROMATIC PASSING TONES

COMBINED SCALE/ARPEGGIO

PASSING MINOR +7: ii - V formula

FINDING THE CHROMATICS: Emphasis of 3rds and 7ths not in the key.

ALTERED DOMINANT NINTH: Skip from 3rd to ♭9th.

ALTERED DOMINANT LICK: Uses altered 9ths and ♭13ths.

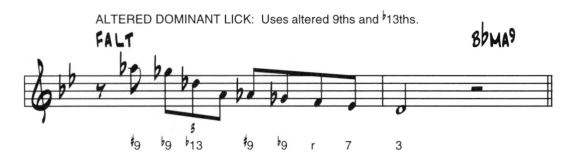

# APPENDIX 6
# Turnaround Lines

APPENDIX 7

# Glossary

**Aeolian** • the diatonic mode constructed from the sixth note of the major scale; equivalent to natural minor; see Chapter 22.

**all-purpose lick** • a chromatic pattern that can be played to any chord or set of chords; see Chapter 23.

**altered dominant cell** • a set of consecutive pitches, based on the diminished scale, containing root, third, seventh, and the altered dominant ninths; see Chapter 12.

**altered dominant chord** • a dominant seventh chord with extensions of a ♭13, ♯9 and/or ♭9, and possibly a ♯11; see Chapter 12.

**altered dominant lick** • a descending triplet arpeggio figure which makes use of the altered dominant tones; see Chapter 12.

**arpeggio** • playing the notes of a chord in melodic sequence; see Chapter 2.

**augmented triad** • contains a major third and an augmented fifth above the root.

**auxiliary tone** • an embellishing note within one step of a chord tone in either direction; see Chapter 8.

**be-bop dominant scale** • a descending pattern consisting of a major scale and both the major and minor sevenths; see Chapter 7.

**blue notes** • the flatted 3rd, 5th and 7th notes of the key; see Chapter 5.

**blues scale** • contains the notes 1, ♭3, 4, ♭5, 5, and ♭7 above a major tonic; see Chapter 5.

**bridge** • the contrasting "B" section of a standard song; also called the release or channel; see Chapter 9.

**cadence** • a progression emphasizing a tonic or concluding a phrase; V-I is the most common cadence; see Chapter 5.

**call and response** • a melodic device, often used in traditional 12-bar blues tunes, where an opening motive (lick) is repeated in the second phrase; see Chapter 7.

**changes** • the chords or chord progression of a song; see Chapter 2.

**chorus** • an improvised solo one time through the progression of a song; see Chapter 6.

**chromatic** • a note or chord not in the key or scale.

**circle of fifths** • a functional relationship of chords by descending perfect fifths; also the relationship of key signatures in which sharps or flats are added as tonics move in successive fifths; see Appendix 3.

**Coltrane turnback** • a substitute turnback progression using chord relationships found in the tune *Giant Steps* (I-♭III-♭VI-V⁷); see Chapter 21.

**combined scale/arpeggio** • a melody containing stepwise motion and occasional skips from one chord tone to the next; see Chapter 6.

**consonant tone** • a note which is in the chord and/or sounds stable with the harmony; see Chapter 2.

**Count Basie ending** • a cadential motive of three chords, usually played by piano, employing a passing diminished seventh chord to connect ii⁷ and tonic harmony (ii-♯ii°-I/iii); see Chapter 13.

**cycle blues** • a 12-bar blues progression featuring various turnaround progressions in the circle of fifths; see Chapter 19.

**deceptive resolution** • occurs when a chord resolves to another that is not expected; typically this term refers to a dominant chord resolving up by step; see Chapter 15.

**decorative chromaticism** • the use of chromatic pitches to embellish, rather than outline chord tones; see Chapter 8.

**diatonic** • a note or chord in the key or scale.

**diminished domain** • a set of four major and minor triads and seventh chords found within the diminished scale, giving rise to a wealth of melodic possibilities; see Chapter 21.

**diminished scale** • alternates whole and half steps, or vice-versa; see Chapter 13.

**diminished seventh chord** • (fully diminished seventh chord) a diminished triad with a diminished seventh above the root; see Chapter 13.

**dominant** • the fifth note of the scale and the chord constructed from that note; see Chapter 5.

**dominant seventh chord** • a major triad with a minor seventh above the root; see Chapter 5.

**Dorian** • the diatonic mode constructed from the second note of a major scale; see Chapter 22.

**embellishing chord** • one which is not functional, but connects two functional chords; see Chapter 13.

**finding the chromatics** • emphasizing the 3rds and 7ths of chords when those notes are not in the key of the song; see Chapter 12.

**formula** • a melodic idea or device so idiomatic to jazz that all players use it frequently; see Chapter 2.

**four-to-one (IV-I) progressions** • found in many standard songs, these interchangeable progressions link subdominant harmony to tonic harmony; see Chapter 13.

**goal note** • a tone which defines the harmony and serves as a guide for that part of the solo; see Chapter 2.

**grace note** • an embellishing tone which leads quickly, by step, into a chord tone; see Ch. 4.

**ground bass** • a minor-key progression emanating from Baroque music, featuring a stepwise, descending bass motion from tonic to dominant; see Chapter 18.

**half-diminished seventh chord** • contains a diminished triad and a minor seventh above the root; see Chapter 11.

**harmonic minor scale** • the natural minor scale with a raised seventh scale degree (leading tone).

**harmonic rhythm** • the rhythm at which the chords change; see Chapter 14.

**head** • the original melody of a song; see Chapter 5.

**interval** • the distance between two notes; intervals have both size (2nd, 3rd, 4th, etc.) and quality (major, minor, perfect, diminished, augmented).

**inversion** • aligning or playing a chord with a note other than the root on the bottom; see Chapter 3.

**Ionian** • the diatonic mode equivalent to major; see Chapter 22.

**isorhythm** • a rhythmic motive which in repetition transcends the meter and bar line; see Chapter 22.

**jazz melodic minor scale** • used for tonic minor harmony, this scale is the ascending form of melodic minor played in both directions; see Chapter 11.

**leading tone** • the seventh note of a major scale (half step below tonic) and the chord constructed on it; see Chapter 5.

**lick** • a short melodic cell, made memorable by its repetition; see Chapter 1.

**Locrian** • the diatonic mode constructed from the seventh note of the major scale; see Ch. 22.

**Lydian** • the diatonic mode constructed from the fourth note of the major scale; see Ch. 22.

**Lydian fourth** • the usage of a raised fourth degree above major or dominant harmony, replacing the more dissonant diatonic fourth; see Chapter 22.

**major scale** • the notes of a major key in successive order; half-steps fall between degrees 3-4 and 7-8.

**major seventh chord** • contains a major triad and a major seventh above the root; see Ch. 4.

**major triad** • consists of a major third and perfect fifth above a chord root; see Chapter 4.

**mediant** • the third note of a scale and the chord built on that note; see Chapter 6.

**melodic minor scale** • the ascending form compares to natural minor, with raised 6th and 7th degrees; the descending form *is* natural minor.

**minor seventh chord** • contains a minor triad

and a minor seventh above the root; see Ch. 6.

**minor triad** • consists of a minor third and perfect fifth above a chord root; see Chapter 6.

**Mixolydian** • the diatonic mode constructed from the fifth note of a major scale; see Ch. 22.

**modal borrowing (interchange)** • the usage of a chord or chords from the parallel mode; see Chapter 17.

**mode** • refers to basing a scale on some pitch other than tonic; in jazz, the diatonic modes are based upon the major scale; see Chapter 22.

**mordent** • an embellishing melodic turn around a chord tone; see Ch. 4.

**natural minor** • a scale using the tones from a minor key, with half-steps falling between 2-3 and 5-6.

**ninth chord** • contains a ninth and a seventh above a triad.

**octatonic scale** • synonymous with diminished scale.

**one-to-six (I-VI) progressions** • refers to a menu of interchangeable harmonies used to connect tonic to a dominant chord built on submediant; see Chapter 16.

**outside playing** • improvisation intentionally employing pronounced dissonance; see Ch. 23.

**parallel chord stream** • improvising to chords a prescribed interval away from the actual changes; see Chapter 23.

**passing tone** • a non-chord tone between chord tones; see Chapter 8.

**pentatonic/blues scale** • consists of the tones 1, 2, ♭3, 3, 5, and 6 above a major tonic; see Ch. 5.

**pentatonic scale** • consisting of five notes; the pentatonic scale used most often in jazz consists of the tones 1, 2, 3, 5, and 6 above a major tonic; see Chapter 21.

**Phrygian** • the diatonic mode constructed from the third note of a major scale; see Chapter 22.

**plagal cadence** • cadential progression from subdominant to tonic; see Ch. 15.

**polyharmony** • improvisation to a triad other than the prevailing chord; the polyharmonic (or

polytonal) triad can usually be analyzed as a set of extensions above the root chord; see Ch. 21.

**polyrhythm** • refers to more than one type of subdivision or metric feel occurring at once; see Chapter 22.

**practice sheet** • notation of the chords and scales contained in the progression of a song; see Chapter 3.

**quartal jazz** • lines based on fourths instead of thirds in arpeggiation; see Chapter 22.

**resolution** • when one chord seems compelled to progress to another, the first chord is said to resolve to the second, and one or more tones within the chord will resolve by step into notes of the other chord; see Chapter 5.

**rhythm changes** • the progression to Gershwin's *I've Got Rhythm*; see Chapter 14.

**scale** • a series of consecutive pitches, with predominant stepwise motion.

**scale/arpeggio turnaround line** • a commonly played ii-V melody line which uses combined scale/arpeggio from the root of the ii chord up to the seventh, followed by a resolution to 3rd of the dominant harmony; see Chapter 9.

**sequence** • a melodic pattern which repeats, and each repetition is transposed by a prescribed interval; see Chapter 6.

**seventh chord** • consists of a triad and a seventh above the root.

**slash chord** • a harmony sounded over a bass note which is either not the root or perhaps not a member of that chord; it is indicated by the chord symbol followed by a diagonal line, then the bass note; see Chapter 22.

**smooth arpeggiation** • using inversion so that two arpeggios can be connected without awkward skips; see Chapter 2.

**solo break** • a melodic statement, usually two measures long, played at the end of a melody without the accompaniment of the rhythm section as a lead-in to a solo; see Chapter 12.

**standard (32-bar) song form** • a tune structured in four 8-bar phrases, the third of which is contrasting (AABA); see Chapter 9.

**step-down progression** • a turnaround progression effecting a modulation down a whole step; see Chapter 17.

**subdominant** • the fourth note of a scale and the chord constructed on it; see Chapter 4.

**submediant** • the sixth note of a scale and the chord constructed on it; see Chapter 6.

**subtonic** • the note a whole step below a tonic and the chord constructed on it; see Chapter 15.

**superimposed triad** • a chord which differs from the prevailing harmony but can be used for improvisation to effect chordal extensions or intentional dissonances; also referred to as *polytonal*; see Chapter 21.

**supertonic** • the second note of a scale and the chord constructed on it; see Chapter 6.

**suspended (sus) chord** • a major or minor triad or seventh chord with a perfect fourth replacing the third of the chord; the resulting sound is quartal in nature; see Chapter 22.

**swing eighth notes** • a performance style where eighth notes are uneven (triplet-like) and most accents fall on the off-beats; see Chapter 1.

**symmetrical chord** • a chord in which any note can be the root; diminished seventh chords and augmented triads are symmetrical; see Ch. 13.

**syncopation** • accenting the off-beats.

**tag ending** • a repeated progression at the end of a song; see Chapter 6.

**tendency tone** • a note requiring resolution; see Chapter 5.

**third-to-flat-ninth (3rd-♭9th) lines** • a melodic device for dominant harmony, especially in minor turnarounds, based on the harmonic minor scale of the tonic; features the 3rd and ♭9 of dominant chord and tendency tone resolution; see Chapter 11.

**third-to-seventh (3rd-7th) interchange** • occurs in blues melodies when the 3rd of the tonic chord goes down a half step to become the 7th of the subdominant chord, and vice versa.

**thirteenth chord** • consists of a triad, with a seventh, ninth and thirteenth above the root; see Chapter 10.

**time** • the conveyance of tempo and rhythm; see Chapter 1.

**tonal music** • where chords and cadence are used functionally, as in traditional, classical music.

**tonic** • the first note of a scale and the chord constructed on it; see Chapter 4.

**tonicise** • to make a chord seem to be a tonic by preceding it with its dominant; see Chapter 10.

**triplet arpeggio** • usually ascending, using a triplet rhythm, and beginning a half step below the root or third of a chord; see Chapter 7.

**tritone** • the interval of a diminished 5th (or augmented 4th); it contains three whole steps; see Chapter 15.

**tritone substituted (Bill Evans) turnaround** • a progression which uses the tritone substituted chords for both ii and $V^7$ (ii-♭vi-♭II-I); see Chapter 21.

**tritone substitution** • refers to the fact that two dominant chords a tritone apart are interchangeable; see Chapter 15.

**turnaround progression** • ii-V or ii-V-I; see Chapter 9.

**turnback progression** • the progression I-$VI^7$-ii-$V^7$, often employed by improvisers at the end of a chorus to "turn back" to the next chorus.

**twelve-bar blues** • the most often played progression in jazz; emphasizes primarily the tonic, subdominant, and dominant chords; see Ch. 7.

**two-chord (ii-chord) substitution** • superimposition of a supertonic chord while a dominant is the prevailing harmony; see Chapter 14.

**"Whisper Not" progression** • a set of chords found in minor keys, effecting a modulation down a perfect fourth; see Chapter 18.

## About the Author

Pianist, composer and educator, **Shelton (Shelly) Berg** is the Chair of Jazz Studies at the University of Southern California, and served as President of the International Association of Jazz Educators (IAJE) from 1996-98. He has enjoyed a long association as pianist and musical director for trombonist Bill Watrous, and has played and recorded with a "Who's Who" of jazz stars. His two solo compact discs are *The Joy* and *The Will*. A finalist in the 1988 Great American Jazz Piano Competition, Shelly's playing has been called "a cross between Bill Evans and Oscar Peterson."

Shelly's compositions and orchestration credits encompass film, television, advertising, and the recording industry. He has worked with orchestras worldwide, and for rock artists including Chicago, Kiss, Richard Marx, Elliott Smith, and the Japanese superstar Yoshiki (X-Japan). He has composed for every major television network, Warner Brothers Films, and most of the largest record labels. Film composer Johnny Mandel raved that Shelly's orchestrations are, "magnificent . . . incredible!"

Shelly has many compositions for jazz ensemble in print with Kendor and other publishers. He has presented educational performances and clinics in over thirty states, as well as in Europe, Japan, Canada, Mexico, and Israel.